O9-CFT-640

Twayne's United States Authors Series

SYLVIA E. BOWMAN, *Editor*

INDIANA UNIVERSITY

Hilda Doolittle

HILDA DOOLITTLE
(H. D.)

By VINCENT QUINN
Brooklyn College

Twayne Publishers, Inc. :: New York

Library of Congress Catalog Card Number: 67-28856

MANUFACTURED IN THE UNITED STATES OF AMERICA BY
UNITED PRINTING SERVICES, INC.
NEW HAVEN, CONN.

Preface

THIS STUDY of Hilda Doolittle began with my curiosity about a poet called "H. D.," who is represented by two or three Imagist poems in virtually every anthology of modern verse. Reading further, I discovered that H. D.'s work was far more extensive than I had expected. Her part in the Imagist movement was only the beginning of a career that continued until her death in 1961. Altogether, she published more than fifteen volumes—poems, novels, essays, and translations from the classics. In addition, she wrote numerous poems that appeared only in periodicals, and—according to Professor Norman Holmes Pearson of Yale University—several lengthy, complete manuscripts as yet unpublished.

I have restricted my discussion to H. D.'s published volumes, omitting her other work because of its inaccessibility. In the first chapter I give an account of her early life and literary apprenticeship. In subsequent chapters the structure and themes of her individual works are closely analyzed. I conclude with a brief evaluation of her total achievement. The sequence of chapters is chronological, except for her prose fiction and her translations, which are best discussed collectively.

VINCENT QUINN

Brooklyn College
City University of New York

Acknowledgments

In writing this study, I have enjoyed the encouragement of many people. In particular, I wish to acknowledge the friendship of my colleague Gloria Glikin, the goodwill of H. D.'s comrade, the historical novelist Bryher, and the courtesy and helpfulness of Professor Norman Holmes Pearson. I am also grateful to the Dean of the Faculties of Brooklyn College for granting me released time in order to work on this book.

Permission to quote from the following publications by H. D. has been generously granted by Professor Norman Holmes Pearson, who holds their copyright, and by the Grove Press for the titles under its imprint:

Bid Me to Live, published by Grove Press, Inc., Copyright © 1960 by Norman Holmes Pearson.

By Avon River. New York: The Macmillan Company, 1949.

Collected Poems of H. D. New York: Liveright Publishing Corp., 1925.

Euripides' Ion, Translated with Notes. Boston: Houghton Mifflin Company, 1937.

Hedylus. Boston: Houghton Mifflin Company, 1928.

Helen in Egypt, published by Grove Press, Inc., Copyright © 1961 by Norman Holmes Pearson.

Hippolytus Temporizes. Boston: Houghton Mifflin Company, 1927.

Palimpsest. Boston: Houghton Mifflin Company, 1926.

Red Roses for Bronze. London: Chatto and Windus, 1931.

Selected Poems of H. D., published by Grove Press, Inc., Copyright © 1957 by Norman Holmes Pearson.

The Flowering of the Rod. New York: Oxford University Press, 1946.

The Walls Do Not Fall. New York: Oxford University Press, 1944.

Tribute to the Angels. New York: Oxford University Press, 1945.

I am also grateful for permission to quote from *Tribute to Freud* by H. D. Copyright © 1956 by Pantheon Books, Inc. Reprinted by permission of Random House, Inc.

Contents

Chronology

1886 September 10, Hilda Doolittle born in Bethlehem, Pennsylvania. Her father, Charles Leander Doolittle, was Director of the Sayre Observatory and Professor of Mathematics and Astronomy at Lehigh University.

1895 Family moved to Philadelphia when her father joined the faculty of the University of Pennsylvania.

1896 Father appointed Flower Professor of Astronomy and the first Director of Flower Observatory at the University of Pennsylvania.

1901 H. D. made the acquaintance of Ezra Pound.

1904 Entered Bryn Mawr College. One of her classmates was the poet Marianne Moore.

1906 Withdrew from college because of poor health. For the next five years, lived with family and began to work seriously at writing.

1911 Traveled in Europe; decided to reside in England.

1913 Married Richard Aldington, Imagist poet who later became a well-known novelist, essayist, and translator. Made her first appearance in *Poetry Magazine*, signing her poems simply "H. D., Imagiste."

1916 *Sea Garden*, poems; *Choruses from Iphigenia in Aulis*, a translation; became the assistant editor of *The Egoist*, replacing her husband who entered the army. Held this position until 1917, when succeeded by T. S. Eliot.

1918 Brother killed in action in France. Met Winifred Ellerman (the historical novelist Bryher) who became intimate friend and benefactor.

1919 Daughter Perdita born; separated from Aldington; father died. *Choruses from the Iphigenia in Aulis and the Hippolytus*, a translation.

1920 Traveled in Greece with Bryher.

1921 *Hymen*, a volume of poems.

1922 Traveled in America with Bryher.

1923 Traveled in Egypt with Bryher. Settled in Switzerland but spent some time in London each year. Lived in London during World War II.

1924 *Heliodora and Other Poems.*

1925 *Collected Poems of H. D.*

1926 *Palimpsest*, a novel.

1927 *Hippolytus Temporizes*, a verse drama.

1928 *Hedylus*, a novel.

1931 *Red Roses for Bronze*, a volume of poems.

1933-1934 Under psychoanalysis by Freud.

1936 *The Hedgehog*, tale for children.

1937 *Euripides' Ion*, translation and commentary.

1938 Divorced from Aldington. Received the annual Helen Haire Levinson Prize of *Poetry Magazine.*

1944 *The Walls Do Not Fall*, the first of a trilogy of war poems.

1945 *Tribute to the Angels*, the second of the trilogy.

1946 *The Flowering of the Rod*, the third of the trilogy.

1949 *By Avon River*, a poem about Shakespeare and an essay celebrating the poets of the English Renaissance.

1956 *Tribute to Freud*, an impressionistic account of her psychoanalysis by Freud.

1957 *Selected Poems of H. D.*

1959 Received the Brandeis University Creative Arts Award for Poetry.

1960 *Bid Me to Live*, a novel. First woman to receive the Award of Merit Medal for Poetry of the American Academy of Arts and Letters.

1961 *Helen in Egypt*, a poem. September 28, died in Zurich, Switzerland.

Hilda Doolittle

CHAPTER 1

The Early Years

HILDA DOOLITTLE'S father, Charles Leander Doolittle, was born in Indiana in 1843, of a Protestant family that had come to the Middle West from New England. After serving in the Civil War, he married and worked as a surveyor for the United States Northern Boundary Commission. In 1874, he took a degree in civil engineering at the University of Michigan. A year later his wife died, leaving him with two sons and a daughter.

The father brought his family east to Bethlehem, Pennsylvania, following his appointment in 1875 as Professor of Mathematics and Astronomy at Lehigh University. There, a few years later, he became the director of the Sayre Observatory. In 1882, he married Helen Eugenie Woole—a descendant, according to H. D., of a member of the "mystical Protestant order, called the Unitas Fratrum, the Bohemian or Moravian Brotherhood"[1] that had left Germany in the eighteenth century in search of religious toleration and had settled in Bethlehem, Pennsylvania. Three children were born of this second marriage: Hilda, the poet, in 1886; a sister who died in childhood; and a brother who was killed in action in World War I.

In 1895, Professor Doolittle joined the faculty of the University of Pennsylvania, and the family moved to Philadelphia. A year later he was appointed Flower Professor of Astronomy and Director of Flower Observatory. He remained at this post until his retirement in 1912, achieving eminence for his research into the variation of terrestrial latitude. He was succeeded as director of the Observatory by his son Eric, H. D.'s half-brother.

These academic achievements did not make childhood happy for H. D., who seems to have found family life restrained and even severe. The home was dominated by her father, the middle-aged astronomer. She later recalled the scene:

> My father's study was lined with books. . . . There was one picture, a photograph of Rembrandt's Dissection, and a skull on the top of my father's highest set of shelves. There was a white owl under a bell-jar. I could sit on the floor with a doll or a folder of paper dolls, but I must not speak to him when he was writing at his table. What he was "writing" was rows and rows of numbers, but I could then scarcely distinguish the shape of a number from a letter, or know which was which. I must not speak to my father when he lay stretched out on the couch, because he worked at night and so must not be disturbed when he lay down on the couch and closed his eyes by day.[2]

She remembered his scolding the children for using his magnifying glass: "It was understood, I thought, that you did not disturb *anything* on my table."[3] In retrospect, H. D. thought that her father had been like "New England, though he does not live there and was not born there. He comes from those Puritan fathers who wear high peaked hats in the Thanksgiving numbers of magazines. They fought with Indians and burned witches."[4]

Her mother was disturbing in a different way: she was not distant but she seemed inaccessible. Later, H. D. remembered thinking that "the trouble is, she knows so many people and they come and interrupt. And besides that, she likes my brother better. If I stay with my brother, become part almost of my brother, perhaps I can get nearer to *her*. But one can never get near enough, or if one gets near, it is because one has measles or scarlet fever."[5] It was perhaps H. D.'s insecurity about her mother's affection that prompted Freud many years later to tell her that she had come to Vienna hoping to find her mother, who had spent her honeymoon there.[6]

Also during her psychoanalysis with Freud, H. D. pictured herself during her early years as "a girl between two boys; but, ironically, it was wispy and mousey, while the boys were glowing and gold. It was not pretty, they said. Then they said it was pretty—but suddenly, it shot up like a weed. They said, surprised, 'She is really very pretty, but isn't it a pity she's so tall?' "[7] During these years she attended local public and private schools; in 1904, she entered Bryn Mawr, where one of her classmates was the poet Marianne Moore. Unfortunately, H. D. was forced to withdraw from college during her sophomore year because of poor health. For the next five years she lived at home, studying and devoting herself seriously to writing. Many years afterward, she recalled this literary apprenticeship:

> . . . of course, I scribbled a bit, adolescent stuff. My first real serious (and I think, in a way, successful) verses were some translations I did of Heine (before I was seriously dubbed "Imagist"). I think they were probably very lyrical in their small way, but of course I destroyed everything. I did a little verse—translation of the lyric Latin poets at Bryn Mawr, vaguely, but nothing came of them. I do not think I even submitted them to the college paper. I do recall, however, how somewhat shocked I was at Bryn Mawr to be flunked quite frankly in English. . . . I suppose that was one of the spurs toward a determination to self-expression. . . . I scribbled later, just before coming "abroad," a half dozen rather free verses that might have been *vers libre*, but I had never heard of *vers libre* till I was "discovered" later by Ezra Pound.[8]

During these years, the focal point of H. D.'s reading was Greek and Latin literature—at first in translation and later in the original. In 1960, she replied to an inquiry about her early interest in the classics: "You are right about the Nietzsche and Walter Pater. But we started earlier with Hawthorne's Tanglewood Tales and all fairy tales. There was the usual school routine, Keats, Shelley, Byron, Swinburne out of school—and some of the Greek (derivative) of Oscar Wilde. . . . I read and re-read as a school-girl *The Last Days of Pompeii* of Bulwer-Lytton—read Landor later in England. . . . Perhaps, as my father and half brother were astronomers, the *names*, Venus, Mercury, and so on, were subconsciously potent, though *consciously* the fairy-tales were nearer. Yes, I read a very little Greek and what possible translations there were—Gilbert Murray's prose rather than his poetry."[9] Perhaps unknown to H. D., her classicism coincided with a remarkable revival of interest in Greek and Latin literature—a revival discussed most helpfully in Douglas Bush's *Mythology and the Romantic Tradition in English Poetry.*[10] In her case, the appeal of the classics was principally the evocation of a distant world, more lovely than the one she knew.

She was encouraged in her classical studies by Ezra Pound, who exercised the strongest influence upon her development as a poet. She first met Pound in 1901, at a friend's Halloween party. H. D. was then fifteen; Pound was only a year older but precocious and already a rare personality. Living near each other and sharing a fondness for literature, they became good friends. William Carlos Williams has written amusingly of being taken by Pound to meet Hilda and her family in 1905:

> From the Penn campus we took the cross-country trolleys of those days and were there in no time. Hilda, Professor Doolittle's youngest daughter by his second wife, was the attraction: at least she was what Pound led me there to see. It certainly wasn't to look through a telescope. There were plenty of stories about that too, and Dr. Doolittle's studious, careful measurements of the earth's oscillation on its axis in turning. A tall, gaunt man who seldom even at table focused upon anything nearer, literally, than the moon. Mrs. Doolittle, considerably younger than he, would silence everyone with a look when she found her husband prepared to talk. He, looking above the heads of those sitting opposite him, would state what he had to say, after which the children and we others having waited decorously to find out if that was the end, would go on talking.
>
> Hilda, tall, blond and with a long jaw but gay blue eyes was, I think, much like her father, though I never saw her pay him any particular attention.
>
> There was about her that which is found in wild animals at times, a breathless impatience, almost a silly unwillingness to come to the point. She had a young girl's giggle and shrug which somehow in one so tall and angular seemed a little absurd. She fascinated me, not for her beauty, which was unquestioned if bizarre to my sense, but for a provocative indifference to rule and order which I liked. She dressed indifferently, almost sloppily and looked to a young man, not inviting—she had nothing of that—but irritating, with a smile.
>
> Ezra was wonderfully in love with her and I thought exaggerated her beauty ridiculously. To me she was just a good guy and I enjoyed, uncomfortably, being with her.[11]

Pound, pleased to be the tutor of so engaging a pupil, guided her reading and commented upon her earliest writing. Years afterward, she remembered that "Ezra Pound was very kind and used to bring me (literally) armfuls of books to read. Among others, there were some rather old de luxe volumes of Renaissance Latin poets. I was happy with those because the Latin was easy yet held the authentic (though diluted) flavor of the overworked and sometimes slavishly copied Latin and Greek originals. I did a few poems that I don't think Ezra liked . . . but later he was beautiful about my first authentic verses."[12]

Their relationship was interrupted in 1908, when Pound left for Europe, but it was resumed three years later when H. D. also went abroad. Her announced intention was to visit the Continent on a summer holiday with friends. However, at the end of the summer, she wrote to her family that she would like to live in England. Her father gave his approval and promised to send her a small allowance. Thus began her expatriation that lasted until her death in Switzerland in 1961.

From the standpoint of establishing herself as a poet, H. D.'s moving to England in the fall of 1911 would at first glance seem inopportune, for she left just before the birth of a new era for American verse. A year later, in October, 1912, *Poetry: A Magazine of Verse* appeared in Chicago under the editorship of Harriet Monroe. In fact, however, H. D.'s move was most fortunate. It gave her personal independence and brought her in touch with other poets who shared her stylistic interests. Moreover, in a short time, she gained a reputation both in England and in America—ironically, through the publication of her poems in *Poetry*.

This happy conjunction of events was due largely to the efforts of her old friend Ezra Pound. By 1911, he felt at home in England and was vigorously propagating his cultural enthusiasms. He knew many editors, publishers, and writers; he was a close friend of William Butler Yeats. As usual, his eye was always cocked for new talent. He encouraged young writers to free themselves from subservience to the immediate past: "As for the nineteenth century, with all respect to its achievements, I think we shall look back upon it as a rather messy, blurry sort of a period, a rather sentimentalistic, mannerish sort of a period."[13] For the future, he wanted poetry "that a grown man could read without groans of ennui, or without having to have it cooed into his ear by a flapper."[14] Believing that poets are the "antennae of the race,"[15] he warned: "It is as important for the purpose of thought to keep language efficient as it is in surgery to keep tetanus bacilli out of one's bandages."[16] Specifically, Pound opposed the genteel, verbose diction, the metrical regularity, the explicit didacticism, and the sentimentality of poems being published in established magazines like *Scribner's* and *The Atlantic*. To his ear, they sounded like third-class versions of Longfellow,

Tennyson, and Swinburne. His corrective was to insist upon economical diction, fresh images, purposeful irregularity in rhythm, and the avoidance of sermonizing.

The launching of *Poetry* gave Pound an opportunity to promote his cause. He recognized at once that this magazine might mean a turning point for modern poetry, because it had financial support and because it was devoted exclusively to verse. In his view, the only uncertain element was the courage of the editor. As soon as he heard of the plan to start the magazine, he began a correspondence with Harriet Monroe, and in August, 1912, he put the matter to her squarely:

> Can you teach the American poet that poetry *is* an *art*, an art with a technique, with media, an art that must be in constant flux, a constant change of manner, if it is to live? Can you teach him that it is not a pentametric echo of the sociological dogma printed in last year's magazines? . . . Are you for American poetry or for poetry? The latter is more important, but it is important that America should boost the former, provided that it don't [*sic*] mean a blindness to the art. The glory of any nation is to produce art that can be exported without disgrace to its origin.[17]

Apparently Miss Monroe replied satisfactorily and, in turn, saw some advantage in associating her magazine with the dynamic American impresario, for the first issue—October, 1912—carried this stately announcement: "Mr. Ezra Pound, the young Philadelphia poet whose recent distinguished success in London led to wide recognition in his own country, authorizes the statement that at present such of his poetic work as receives magazine publication in America will appear exclusively in *Poetry*."[18] In the second issue there was notice that Pound had won a strategic position for his literary crusade: "Mr. Ezra Pound has consented to act as foreign correspondent of *Poetry*, keeping its readers informed of the present interests of the art in England, France and elsewhere."[19]

Pound used his new position to publicize a group of poets whose outlook he shared. The work of this group of English and American writers—and membership was neither fixed nor formal—has come to be known as Imagism. Pound was its promoter, and its most representative member was H. D. The complicated evolution of the meaning of Imagism has been traced in two books: in Glenn Hughes' *Imagism and the Imagists* (1931),[20] and in Stanley K. Coffman's *Imagism: A Chapter for the History of Modern Poetry* (1951).[21] Since it is only H. D.'s role in the movement that concerns this study, Coffman's general definition will suffice: "Imagism refers to the theory and practice of a group of poets who, between 1912 and 1917, joined in reaction against the careless technique and extra-poetic values of much nineteenth-century verse."[22]

Once in London, H. D. renewed her friendship with Pound, and through him she became acquainted with the other poets associated with Imagism: Ford Madox Ford, F. S. Flint, Allen Upward, John Gould Fletcher, and—most important—Richard Aldington. H. D. and Aldington discovered that they both were trying to express in their own poetry the spare beauty they admired in Greek and Latin verse. Pound, seeing in their work the qualities he had been recommending for poetry generally, shaped the Imagist movement around them.

He placed three poems by Aldington in the second issue of *Poetry* (November, 1912) and added a teasing note associating Aldington with the still unknown movement: "Mr. Richard Aldington is a young British poet, one of the 'Imagistes,' a group of ardent Hellenists who are pursuing interesting experiments in *vers libre*; trying to attain in English certain subtleties of cadence of the kind which Mallarmé and his followers have studied in French. Mr. Aldington has published little as yet, and nothing in America."[23]

For Pound, the fourth issue of *Poetry* (January, 1913) was a greater victory. He placed three poems by H. D.—she called them "my first authentic verses,"[24]—which he persuaded her to sign simply "H. D., Imagiste." Behind Pound's triumph lay a campaign that, fortunately, can be reconstructed. Aldington has told in his autobiography how the poems were selected and how H. D.'s appellation was decided upon at a meeting over tea:

> I have no exact memory of what was said at this bun-shop meeting, but I do remember that H. D. looked very much pleased by the praise Ezra generously gave her poems. I didn't like his insistence that the poems should be signed "H. D. Imagist," because it sounded a little ridiculous. And I think H. D. disliked it too. But Ezra was a bit of a czar in a small but irritating way, and he had the bulge on us, because it was only through him that we could get our poems into Harriet Monroe's *Poetry*, and nobody else at that time would look at them. (My impression is that even

> so Ezra had to bully Miss Monroe to get her to accept this "new" poetry.) So we had to give in.
>
> If I am not mistaken, these poems of H. D.'s were the first to appear with the Imagist label. Three of mine . . . had appeared a month or two before without the label, though Ezra afterwards included them in the first Imagist anthology. I think this fact . . . lends considerable support to those who say the Imagist movement was H. D., and H. D. the Imagist movement.[25]

H. D.'s poems were "Hermes of the Ways," "Priapus" (called "Orchard" in *Collected Poems*), and "Epigram" (not included in *Collected Poems*). In *Poetry* they were ambiguously headed "Verses, Translations, and Reflections from 'The Anthology.'" Pound had sent them to Harriet Monroe in October, 1912, accompanied by his strongest endorsement: "I've had luck again, and am sending you some *modern* stuff by an American, I say modern, for it is in the laconic speech of the Imagistes, even if the subject is classic. At least H. D. has lived with these things since childhood, and knew them before she had any book-knowledge of them. This is the sort of American stuff that I can show here and in Paris without its being ridiculed. Objective—no slither; direct—no excessive use of adjectives, no metaphors that won't permit examination. It's straight talk, straight as the Greek! And it was only by persistence that I got to see it at all."[26]

As Pound hoped, the poems created a stir. Their charm was irresistible, and the mystery of the author's identity aroused curiosity. A note stated merely that "H. D., *Imagiste*! is an American lady resident abroad, whose identity is unknown to the editor."[27] This notice established the association of H. D. with Imagism that still persists, even though her career outdistanced the movement by more than forty years. However, in terms of these three poems, the association was entirely just. For example, "Priapus" illustrates both H. D.'s lyrical gift and the important characteristics of Imagism: brevity, concrete imagery, and flexible versification. The poem is a plea that nature withhold its beauty from us since beauty is inevitably followed by decay:

> O rough-hewn
> god of the orchard,
> I bring you an offering—
> do you, alone unbeautiful,
> son of the god,
> spare us from loveliness:

these fallen hazel-nuts,
stripped late of their green sheaths,
grapes, red-purple,
their berries
dripping with wine,
pomegranates already broken,
and shrunken figs
and quinces untouched,
I bring you as offering.

(*Collected Poems*, 40-41)

It was after reading these poems that Amy Lowell exclaimed, "Why, I, too, am an Imagiste!"[28] and began to make inquiries about the movement that before long she was to dominate.

Encouraged by his success in placing H. D.'s poems, Pound intensified his campaign. In the same issue of *Poetry* in which she made her debut, he contributed an essay entitled "*Status Rerum*" in which he praised the *Imagistes* as writers who took precision as their watchword and who were "in opposition to the numerous and unassembled writers who busy themselves with dull and interminable effusions."[29] The issue of March, 1913, contained a report by F. S. Flint of an interview with an Imagist; it was in fact a statement of policy by Pound.[30] In the same issue, Pound also contributed a piece called "A Few Don'ts by an Imagiste."[31] In both of these essays he reiterated the cardinal aims of Imagism: precision, economy, concreteness, and stylistic innovation.

The culmination of Pound's efforts was the publication in 1914 of *Des Imagistes: An Anthology*.[32] It contained six poems by H. D., as well as selections by Aldington, F. S. Flint, Skipwith Cannell, Amy Lowell, William Carlos Williams, James Joyce, Pound, Ford Madox Ford, Allen Upward, and John Cournos. With the appearance of this anthology, Pound believed that he had succeeded in making "it possible for a few poets who were not over-producing, to reach an audience."[33] But the collection also marked the end of Pound's interest in the movement. He felt that the influence of Amy Lowell, who had come to England to meet her fellow Imagists and to promote their cause, was becoming excessive. He complained that she would turn Imagism "into a democratic beer-garden . . . by making it mean *any* writing of *vers libre*."[34] She prevailed nonetheless, and Pound, predicting the collapse of the movement into prolixity, went on to other struggles.

In the meanwhile, H. D. and Aldington were married in October, 1913. As poets, admirers of classical civilization, and enemies of middle-class life, they seemed completely congenial. After touring Italy, they took a flat in Kensington and spent much time in art galleries and the British Museum. In his *Autobiography*, John Cournos described their life at this time:

> H. D. (Hilda Doolittle) and Richard Aldington, newly married, lived in Holland Place Chambers, not many yards from my lodgings, and Ezra Pound, on his marriage, took up his abode with his Dorothy just across the landing from the Aldingtons. A little further in one direction was Mrs. Shakespear's house (Olivia Shakespear, Pound's mother-in-law), and in another house a little further down the Hueffers (Ford Madox Ford) lived. . . . I saw particularly a great deal of the Aldingtons, who . . . went out of their way to be nice to me. . . . Here were two poets, man and woman, who were happy together and worked together; at this time, at any rate, their relation seemed to me to be an ideal one.[35]

Amy Lowell, in England in 1914 to meet the Imagist group, had the same impression; she reported to Harriet Monroe that "the great thing which my summer has done for me is bringing me the intimacy of the Aldingtons. They are a perfectly charming young couple."[36]

That same year the war began, but some time passed before its impact was felt by this group of poets. For a while, literary activity went on as usual. Amy Lowell devoted her abundant managerial talent to making America and England more appreciative of Imagism. Although Ezra Pound continued to read disaster in her casual attitude toward the principles of the movement, the Aldingtons were grateful for the boost she gave them. She arranged for Houghton Mifflin to publish an annual Imagist anthology containing selections from both American and English poets. The title and the roster of contributors involved difficult negotiations with Pound, but in 1915 the first volume appeared as *Some Imagist Poets: An Anthology*.[37] The Americans included were H. D., John Gould Fletcher, and Miss Lowell; the English contributors were Aldington, F. S. Flint, and D. H. Lawrence. H. D. was represented by "The Pool," "The Garden," "Sea Lily," "Sea Iris," "Sea Rose," "Oread," and "Orion Dead."

An important feature of this anthology was the prefatory statement listing the "essentials of all great poetry" as understood by the contributors. Known as the Imagist Credo, it is specific enough to indicate the distinguishing spirit of the group and yet sufficiently general to transcend minor differences and to elicit the widest support:

1. To use the language of common speech, but to employ always the *exact* word, not the nearly-exact, nor the merely decorative word.
2. To create new rhythms—as the expression of new moods—and not to copy old rhythms, which merely echo old moods. We do not insist upon "free verse" as the only method of writing poetry. We fight for it as for a principle of liberty. We believe that the individuality of a poet may often be better expressed in free verse than in conventional forms. In poetry, a new cadence means a new idea.
3. To allow absolute freedom in the choice of subject. It is not good art to write badly about aeroplanes and automobiles; nor is it necessarily bad art to write well about the past. We believe passionately in the artistic value of modern life, but we wish to point out that there is nothing so uninspiring nor so old-fashioned as an aeroplane of the year 1911.
4. To present an image (hence the name, imagist). We are not a school of painters, but we believe that poetry should render particulars exactly and not deal in vague generalities, however magnificent and sonorous. It is for this reason that we oppose the cosmic poet, who seems to us to shirk the real difficulties of his art.
5. To produce poetry that is hard and clear, never blurred nor indefinite.
6. Finally, most of us believe that concentration is of the very essence of poetry.[38]

In 1916, H. D.'s literary career entered a new phase of activity and responsibility. Her first book, *Sea Garden*, containing twenty-seven poems, was published. In addition, she assumed her husband's position as literary editor of *The Egoist*, a monthly journal of opinion. The issue of June, 1916, listed both Richard Aldington and H. D. as assistant editors but gave notice that "Mr. Aldington will shortly be called up for military service and during his absence the assistant-editorship of *The Egoist* will be taken over by H. D. (Mrs. Richard Aldington)."[39]

H. D. took her editorial responsibilities with the utmost seriousness, in keeping with her belief in the supreme importance of literature. Her attitude may be deduced from the note which she sent to William Carlos Williams about a poem he had submitted:

> I trust you will not hate me for wanting to delete from your poem all the flippancies. The reason I want to do this is that the beautiful lines are so very beautiful—so in the tone and spirit of your *Postlude*—(which to me stands, a Nike, supreme among your poems). I think there is *real* beauty—and real beauty is a rare and sacred thing in this generation. . . .
>
> I don't know what you think but I consider this business of writing a very sacred thing!—I think you have the "spark"—am sure of it, and when you speak *direct* are a poet. I feel in the hey-ding-ding touch running through your poem a derivative tendency which, to me, is not you—not your very self. It is as if you were *ashamed* of your Spirit, ashamed of your inspiration!—as if you mocked at your own song. It's very well to *mock* at yourself—it is a spiritual sin to mock at your inspiration.[40]

From 1917 until the Armistice, the Aldingtons suffered intensely from the war. Richard kept shuttling between active duty at the front and brief furloughs at home. H. D. kept their flat at Mecklenburgh Square but was exhausted by her work and the uncertainties of their life. In March, 1917, D. H. Lawrence wrote to Amy Lowell that "Hilda Aldington seems very sad and suppressed, everything is wrong."[41] Three months later, *The Egoist* announced that H. D.'s place would be assumed by T. S. Eliot. In the fall, Lawrence and his German wife moved to London in a bitter frame of mind after being required by the security police to leave Cornwall. They had been suspected of planning to send signals from the shore to German ships. Fortunately, as Lawrence later wrote to Amy Lowell, "Hilda like an angel came to the rescue and lent us her room."[42] This arrangement was temporary, but the Lawrences remained in the neighborhood and frequently gathered at the Aldingtons' flat. An impression of H. D. and Aldington in this setting—remarkably similar to the one presented by H. D. later in her novel *Bid Me to Live*—has been written by Brigit Patmore:

> In the Aldingtons' room the apricot-coloured walls were lit by candles, dark blue curtains covered the windows. A table had a large red platter heaped with fruit, and a huge plate held whatever could be got of ham and sausages, and there was bread and

wine. . . . Everyone burned with a different incandescence. . . . Hilda, a swaying sapling almost destroyed by tempests, all the blueness of flame gone into her large distracted eyes. . . . Richard flickered with the desperate gaiety of the soldier on leave and unresolved pain. He had the most robust body and therefore its broad strength showed none of our febrile agitations.[43]

Also in 1917, the final edition of *Some Imagist Poets* appeared. H. D. reassured Amy Lowell that her decision to end the series was correct: "I think we all feel the same about the Anthology. It was splendid for the three years—but its work, as you say, is finished—its collective work that is. Each of us has gained by the brother-ship but we are all developing along different lines—all of us who are developing."[44] The three annual anthologies had attracted considerable attention. The six contributors were then in a position, as H. D. said, to follow their own line independently.

Toward the end of the war, H. D.'s brother was killed in action in France and her flat was bombed, although no one was hurt. Then the Armistice was signed, and Aldington returned home safely; but H. D. remained in downcast spirits and poor health. D. H. Lawrence reported to Amy Lowell: ". . . saw Richard, who was on leave. He is very fit, looking forward to peace and freedom. Hilda also is in town—not so very well. She is going to have another child, it appears. [She had previously lost a child by miscarriage.] I hope she will be all right. Perhaps she can get more settled, for her nerves are very shaken: and perhaps the child will soothe her and steady her. I hope it will."[45]

Lawrence's hopefulness was misplaced, because H. D.'s melancholy was caused by a worry that pregnancy could only aggravate—the collapse of her marriage. Aldington later explained in his autobiography that "through my own folly or worse, I had got my personal life into a tragical mess, which added to my difficulties, and resulted in separation from H. D."[46] The trouble seems to have been caused by his attachment to Dorothy "Arabella" Yorke, who lived in the Aldingtons' building and who is patently the prototype of the character Bella in H. D.'s novel *Bid Me to Live*. H. D. and Aldington parted in 1919, but were not divorced until 1938. Aldington became a well-known man of letters: poet, novelist, biographer, translator, and editor.

For H. D., the compensating event of 1918 was her meeting

with Bryher, the daughter of the wealthy English businessman Sir John Ellerman. Named Winifred, she chose to be called simply "Bryher" (one of the Scilly Isles) in order to assert her independence of her family. She has become a renowned author of historical novels, but in 1918 she was mainly dreaming of escaping from her parents. In her autobiography *The Heart to Artemis* she has written of her introduction to H. D.'s poetry: "There will always be one book among all the others that makes us aware of ourselves; for me, it is *Sea Garden* by H. D. I learned it by heart from cover to cover."[47] She then wrote to H. D., and they met. H. D. liked her; for Bryher it was a fervid encounter: "I had a friend at last who talked to me about poetry and did not laugh at my meager attempts at writing. (Not that I thought them meager at the time!) It was my first real contact with an artist, and H. D. was the most beautiful figure that I have ever seen in my life, with a face that came directly from a Greek statue and, almost to the end, the body of an athlete."[48]

In the early months of 1919, H. D. was in great distress. Besides being pregnant and separated from her husband, she was stricken with double pneumonia. Then news arrived of the death of her father. Fortunately, both she and the baby, a girl named Perdita, survived. During all these difficulties, her new friend was magnanimous. As H. D. later acknowledged, "The material and spiritual burden of pulling us out of danger fell upon a young woman whom I had only recently met—anyone who knows me knows who this person is. Her pseudonym is Bryher and we all call her Bryher. If I got well, she would herself see that the baby was protected and cherished and she would take me to a new world, a new life, to the land, spiritually of my predilection, geographically of my dreams. We would go to Greece, it could be arranged."[49]

When H. D. recovered, Bryher kept all her promises. For a while, they and the baby lived together in Kensington. In the spring of 1920, the two women journeyed to Greece; the following year they visited America, traveling cross-country to California. In 1923, they explored ancient monuments in Egypt. After the tour of Egypt, H. D. settled in Switzerland. There she worked at her writing and enjoyed the countryside with her daughter and Bryher, who lived nearby. Whenever Switzerland became monotonous, she took vacations, often making lengthy visits to London and Paris.

In 1925, *Collected Poems of H. D.* appeared, containing her three previously published volumes—*Sea Garden* (1916), *Hymen* (1921), and *Heliodora and Other Poems* (1924)—and several translations from the Greek. The publication of *Collected Poems* brought the first phase of H. D.'s career to a close and is an appropriate place to end this biographical account. Her life remained active, of course, for thirty-five more years, but for the purpose of this study, no further emphasis need be placed upon personal details. By 1925, the experiences that occasioned and tempered almost all her writing had occurred. The subsequent years, excepting those spent in London during World War II, seem uneventful by comparison. It was as though, following the dissolution of her marriage, she returned to the retired life she had known between leaving Bryn Mawr in 1906 and going abroad in 1911. She joined no literary groups but steadfastly kept on with her writing. Thirteen volumes—verse, novels, drama, essays, translations—were published during the remaining years. In them, incidents and impressions from the earlier years were explored (often in a classical disguise) in a search for their deepest meaning. With the passage of time, her work grew more complex, but it was a complexity caused by her more thoroughly probing the same subjects. Even the few later events that she wrote about—her psychoanalysis with Freud and her experiences during the Battle of Britain—are interesting mainly because they add new dimensions to her old concerns. H. D.'s work is like a spiral: a continuous circuit over the same area. Her subjects are few, but her understanding of them changes as she views them from different heights.

CHAPTER 2

Collected Poems

THE PUBLICATION of *Collected Poems of H. D.* (1925)[1] established H. D.'s reputation. Included were her first three volumes of verse—*Sea Garden* (1916), *Hymen* (1921), and *Heliodora and Other Poems* (1924)—as well as her translations from Euripides' *Iphigenia, Hippolytus,* and *Ion,* and from the opening section of *The Odyssey.* As the work of H. D.'s early years, *Collected Poems* creates a unified impression. Although the poems vary in subject and theme, they form a body of verse easily distinguished from her later work—for example, from her next volume of lyrics, *Red Roses for Bronze* (1931).

Collected Poems has done H. D. only one disservice: the title suggests the end rather than the beginning of her career. Although five volumes of verse appeared subsequently, from *Red Roses for Bronze* in 1931 to *Helen in Egypt* in 1961, the collection made it easy for readers to overlook them. Thus it supported the already established notion that H. D. and Imagism were synonymous. Because Imagism was defunct by 1925, H. D.'s work was considered finished also. Regrettably, anthologists have sustained this false impression by representing her exclusively as an Imagist. Only Norman Holmes Pearson in his edition of her *Selected Poems* (1957) offers a fair sampling of her entire range.[2]

However, in one respect this emphasis upon *Collected Poems* has been justified. Although H. D. published volumes of verse for more than thirty-five years after the appearance of the collection, she produced none better than this one. The effort to call attention to her later work must not overshadow the fact that *Collected Poems* contains her finest verse. It possesses the intensity that results from clear vision, creativity, and craftsmanship. These poems were firmly conceived and lovingly shaped. Written in free verse, they are triumphs of precision and control, unmarred either by carelessness or preciosity. Their rhythm is rhetorical, suited to the emphasis of intense speech; their diction is both concrete and richly connotative. Allowing for some weak spots in a collection of eighty-five poems, the reader generally finds that the book lives up to Ezra Pound's earliest praise of her work: "Objective—no slither; direct—no excessive use of adjectives, no metaphors that won't permit examination."[3]

The devotion to poetry necessary for such an accomplishment is evident in the previously quoted letter written by H. D. to William Carlos Williams about his poem "March." She regarded poetry as sacred, and she endeavored to rise to its demands. Two people who knew her intimately, Richard Aldington and Bryher, have both written of her respect for artistry. Aldington says in his autobiography that her "craftsmanship was the result of infinite pains. Version after version of a poem was discarded by H. D. in the search for perfection, and the pruning was ruthless. I had thought I was fairly exacting, but I was staggered by this relentless artistic conscience. The fervour with which ten generations of Puritan ancestors had sought moral righteousness was here devoted to aesthetic righteousness. I think it significant that H. D. was a close student of St. Paul, but obviously her version of the famous tirade ran: 'Though I speak with the tongue of men and angels and have not style . . . !' "[4] Bryher recalls that once during her early days with H. D., "I interrupted her work and she tore up the page that she had just begun. I collected the fragments humbly, pasted them together and never intruded again."[5]

Recognizing that H. D.'s finest work is in *Collected Poems* involves accepting her place in modern poetry as minor. Splendid as these poems are, they are slight. Their brevity is the sign not only of delicacy and precision but of modest capacity. Their glory is their luminous self-realization: descriptions of nature and expressions of personal longings. They transform the tensions of experience into the paradoxically serene excitement of art. The reader sees his own conflicts reflected in hers and is strengthened by the esthetic harmony that she creates from them. However, he does not find in them the larger intellectual and social concerns of major poetry. The range of subjects and the complexity of mind and feeling found in Yeats, Eliot, Auden, and the great poets of the past define the limits of H. D.'s achievement. Without denigrating her talent in the least, assent must be given to R. P. Blackmur's judgment of her early work: "For the lesser satisfactions alone H. D. remains adequate."[6]

I *H. D.'s Classicism*

The most obvious characteristic of *Collected Poems*—and of H. D.'s work generally—is her interest in ancient Greece. A glance at the table of contents shows that most of the titles are Hellenic: "Oread," "Adonis," "Eurydice," "Thetis," and "Cassandra." More than twenty poems are dramatic monologues by characters either known from classical Greek literature or imagined as having lived in those times. Another twenty are lyrics on Hellenic subjects; five are adaptations of fragments by Sappho, and several that describe nature refer to Grecian landscapes. This Hellenism has, naturally, provided critics and publishers with a convenient tag for H. D.'s work. The epithets "Greek," "classical," and "Hellenic," as well as the related adjectives "cold," "chiselled," "crystalline," and "pure," have been linked so tightly to her name that what began as a compliment has become a cliché. Moreover, even though the association of her work with classical Greece is just, it gives rise to problems that may diminish her reputation unfairly.

The first problem—common to the use of all broad descriptive terms—is the uncertain meaning of "Greek" and "classical." Like "romantic" and "medieval," these designations have been swollen by countless amplifications. As a simple way of summing up diverse elements, they are useful; but they are subject to private meanings. Does "Greek" mean Athens in the time of Pericles, Alexandria in the third century, the Macedonian rites to Dionysos, or Sappho's school for girls on Lesbos? If the reader holds any of these historical references too rigidly, he may be inhospitable to other equally sound ones.

Another problem involves the responsibility of a lyric poet to history and tradition. What degree of authenticity is expected in a lyric about Alexander the Great or Plato? Inaccuracy is a flaw but not the worst one, since the essence of a lyric is the poet's reaction to his subject. This excuse is more relevant when the subject is not historical but mythic or legendary. The general contour of a traditional subject must be respected, of course, in order to prevent the subject from becoming a barrier to communication. For example, Achilles must not be presented as a weakling nor Hector as a traitor. Beyond this requirement, however, the lyric poet has considerable license; he may place traditional characters in novel situations and express unconventional attitudes toward them.

If these caveats are heeded, the reader will be in a better position to enjoy H. D.'s classicism. He will not be upset, as T. B. Swann in *The Classical World of H. D.* seems to be, that "she shaped the classical world to her own temperament."[7] H. D. reacts according to her own temperament, of course; yet she presents no outlandish distortion of classical images. Similarly, the tolerant reader will not be as censorious as Douglas Bush:

> The Greece she dwells in has no real connection with the Greece of historic actuality. Most of her poetry has the air of an exquisitely chiseled reproduction of something, though it is a reproduction of something that never existed. H. D. is a poet of escape. Her refuge is a dream-world of ideal beauty which she calls Greece; her self-conscious, even agonized, pursuit of elusive beauty is quite un-Greek. The fact is that the hard bright shell of H. D.'s poetry partly conceals a soft romantic nostalgia which, however altered and feminized, is that of the Victorian Hellenists.[8]

Discounting Bush's pejorative rhetoric—the elusiveness of his "no real connection," his use of "dream-world" instead of "imagination," and his finding romantic nostalgia "soft"—there remains his implication that lyric poetry should be history. He fails to see that the main issue is not whether the pursuit of elusive beauty is "un-Greek"; it is whether H. D. makes this endeavor plausible in the poem. Similarly, even if she is a "Victorian Hellenist," the potentiality of her verse is not thereby lowered. Obviously, the only true ancient Greeks were the ancient Greeks—and their literature shows how varied they were. History may provide a picture of what they actually were like, but the historian need not be distressed by the impression they make on later poets.

A more temperate and helpful view of H. D.'s classicism is offered by Horace Gregory and Marya Zaturenska in *A History of American Poetry: 1900-1940.* Their remarks refer principally to *Collected Poems,* because they wrote before H. D.'s more meditative poems appeared.

> The Greek temples of H. D. shine with a brilliant, a supernal light, their inhabitants move in a hemisphere almost too delicately sensuous, and they themselves are too modern in sensibility, too nervous in their intensity to be conventionally Attic. Theirs

is not the marmoreal repose and harmony that one usually associates with figures in bas-relief on a Greek urn, for H. D.'s islands are inhabited by spirits who are possessed by that romantic neurosis, the longing for the imagined perfection of Greek attitudes and the eternal solace of the Hellenic dream that haunts the western world, and has often been the source of its finest thinking, action, and poetry. The diction, the sensibility of H. D.'s poetry are strictly modern in external tone and feeling and the poems are clean and straight.[9]

II *Major Themes*

Desire for the Wildness of Nature

Several themes dominate both the classical and non-classical poems of the collection. The most fundamental one is H. D.'s rejection of modern urban life. In "Cities" she grieves over "street after street,/each patterned alike,/no grace to lighten/a single house of the hundred/crowded into one garden-space," houses in which "souls live, hideous yet—/O disfigured, defaced,/with no trace of the beauty/men once held so light." The only consolation she can derive from this scene is the fancy that urban ugliness is perhaps only a phase in the evolution of a new way of life more beautiful than the old "arch upon perfect arch." On the basis of this fancy, she imagines that she and all other lovers of beauty are cells of estheticism destined to germinate a "new beauty of cities" in the drab tissue of modern society. However, she seems to have little confidence in this fancy, for the burden of the poem is sad and alienated.

H. D.'s usual impulse is to abandon the cities in favor of nature. This impulse is fruitful, for she is infinitely more persuasive as an observer and admirer of nature than as a social prophet. Some of her most successful poems are precise and vivid descriptions of natural phenomena. Comment is neither made nor needed; an attitude of respect is conveyed by her alert submission to her subject. Typical of these modest but impeccable poems is "Storm":

> You crash over the trees,
> you crack the live branch—
> the branch is white,
> the green crushed,
> each leaf is rent like split wood.

You burden the trees
with black drops,
you swirl and crash—
you have broken off a weighted leaf
in the wind,
it is hurled out,
whirls up and sinks,
a green stone.

The precise diction of this poem is in keeping with a prime tenet of Imagism. The arresting metaphor at the end—comparing "a weighted leaf" to "a green stone"—also is in accord with the Imagist "credo."

A more forceful metaphor governs "Oread"—also a description of a storm. In this poem the mood of the poet is more apparent than in "Storm":

Whirl up, sea—
whirl your pointed pines,
splash your great pines
on our rocks,
hurl your green over us,
cover us with your pools of fir.

Besides Pound's "In a Station of the Metro," this is the most widely known Imagist poem. Both are paradigms of the movement, for their brevity, non-didacticism, and arresting metaphors demonstrate the correctives that the Imagist poets wished to apply to modern verse.

H. D.'s choice of storms as the subject of these poems is not fortuitous. It represents a characteristic feature of her interest in nature: her pleasure in its untamed aspects. She did not merely prefer nature to the cities; she recognized that some fields are so protected and cultivated that they are as artificial as city-life and deserve equally to be rejected. Her disdain for such sanctuaries is expressed in "Sheltered Garden":

I have had enough.
I gasp for breath.

. . . . .

For this beauty,
beauty without strength,
chokes out life.
I want wind to break,
scatter these pink-stalks,

snap off their spiced heads,
fling them about with dead leaves—
spread the paths with twigs,
limbs broken off,
trail great pine branches,
hurled from some far wood
right across the melon-patch,
break pear and quince—
leave half-trees, torn, twisted
but showing the fight was valiant.

O to blot out this garden
to forget, to find a new beauty
in some terrible
wind-tortured place.

H. D. cherishes natural objects most when they withstand fierce conditions. For example, in the *Sea Garden* section of *Collected Poems*, she pays tribute to sturdy aquatic flowers. The title refers to five poems: "Sea Rose," "Sea Lily," "Sea Poppies," "Sea Violet," and "Sea Iris." She loves these flowers more than the usual garden variety because they endure the assault of wave, wind, and sand. Although these sea flowers are often scarred and broken, they are the more precious for having outlasted danger. The theme and manner of these poems are illustrated by "Sea Poppies":

Amber husk
fluted with gold,
fruited on the sand
marked with a rich grain,

treasure
spilled near the shrub-pines
to bleach on the boulders:

your stalk has caught root
among wet pebbles
and drift flung by the sea
and grated shells
and split conch-shells.

Beautiful, wide-spread,
fire upon leaf,
what meadow yields
so fragrant a leaf
as your bright leaf?

A preference for hardihood governs her poems about people as well as those about nature, about the past as well as the present. Harriet Monroe recognized this quality and was surprised to find it in so cultivated an artist: "The astonishing thing about H. D.'s poetry is the wildness of it—that trait strikes me as I read her whole record in the *Collected Poems*. . . . She is as wild as deer on the mountains. . . . She is never indoors, never even in a tent. . . . She is, in a sense, one of the most civilized, most ultra-refined of poets; and yet never was a poet more unaware of civilization, more independent of its thralls. . . . It would be an interesting speculation to consider how much H. D. owes to the pioneers whom all Americans descend from more or less."[10] The clue to Miss Monroe's riddle about a civilized poet "unaware of civilization" is H. D.'s concept of the term. To her, it is not well-appointed comfort but a combination of sensitivity and toughness, beauty and strength. She admires Greek civilization because it was rugged and out-of-doors—more than is usually supposed. Significantly, after World War I, H. D. took up residence in an Alpine village.

In many poems, she imagines herself as living in more primitive times. The challenge expressed in "Huntress" is typical:

> Come, blunt your spear with us,
> our pace is hot
> and our bare heels
> in the heel-prints—
> we stand tense—do you see—
> are you already beaten
> by the chase?
>
> We lead the pace
> for the wind on the hills,
> the low hill is spattered
> with loose earth—
> our feet cut into the crust
> as with spears.
>
> We climbed the ploughed land,
> dragged the seed from the clefts,
> broke the clod with our heels,
> whirled with a parched cry
> into the woods:

can you come,
can you come,
can you follow the hound trail,
can you trample the hot froth?

Spring up—sway forward—
follow the quickest one,
aye, though you leave the trail
and drop exhausted at our feet.

Likewise, in "Sea Heroes" she praises ancient Greece, "for she gives men as great as the sea,/valorous to the fight,/to battle against the elements and evil." In "Loss," her scorn for ease and compromise is extreme. She imagines herself a member of a small band fighting a powerful enemy. Recognizing the imminence of defeat, she is thankful that the strongest of her comrades has been killed because he will escape humiliation:

I am glad the tide swept you out,
O beloved,
you of all this ghastly host
alone untouched,
your white flesh covered with salt
as with myrrh and burnt iris.

Desire for Comradeship with the Gods

In several poems, H. D. expresses the desire to be a comrade of the gods. She considers the difficulty of achieving this relationship a test of her ardor and, of itself, a strong reason for making the effort. In "The Cliff Temple," she imagines herself "splintered and torn" by the pursuit of an infinitely alluring and elusive god: "Over me the wind swirls./I have stood on your portal/and I know—/you are further than this,/still further on another cliff." She prays in "Sea Gods" to deities who are nowadays regarded as "cut, torn, mangled." Rejecting the scepticism of modern times, she offers a bouquet of violets to her gods and pleads:

For you will come,
you will come,
you will answer our taut hearts,
you will break the lie of men's thoughts,
and cherish and shelter us.

"The God" suggests that her prayer has been answered. She concedes that her faith had been imperiled, that she had wondered: "can he from his portals of ebony/carved with grapes,/turn toward the earth?"

> I even spoke this blasphemy
> in my thoughts:
> the earth is evil,
> given over to evil,
> we are lost.

Then, "in a moment" her faith was confirmed. She felt that the god had become incarnate in the cyclamen flower and that she had been united with him in love:

> beneath my feet, the rocks
> have no weight
> against the rush of cyclamen,
> fire-tipped, ivory-pointed,
> white;
>
> beneath my feet the flat rocks
> have no strength
> against the deep purple flower-embers,
> cyclamen, wine spilled.
>
> . . . .
>
> I pluck the cyclamen,
> red by wine-red,
> and place the petals'
> stiff ivory and bright fire
> against my flesh;
>
> now I am powerless
> to draw back
> for the sea is cyclamen-purple,
> cyclamen-red, colour of the last grapes,
> colour of the purple of the flowers,
> cyclamen-coloured and dark.

The association of the cyclamen and the sea in the final stanza is portentous. It suggests that, following union with the flower-god, the poet feels his presence in the sea. As a trysting-place from which she is "powerless/to draw back," the sea may represent an impulse toward death.

Dedication to Poetry

The intensity that H. D. admired in nature and sought in her relationship with the deity also characterizes her attitude toward poetry. She considers poetry a vocation, and she hopes to use her talent to create an austere beauty. In "Wash of Cold River," a poem serving as the epigraph to *Heliodora*, she rejects intimate thoughts" and "intimate hands" that would share

all the sheer rapture
that I would take
to mould a clear
and frigid statue;

rare, of pure texture,
beautiful space and line,
marble to grace
your inaccessible shrine.

In "Prayer" she asks a goddess or a Muse to "give back the tool,/ the chisel; once we wrought/things not unworthy"; she wishes to use it to fashion the garb of an ancient soldier. Armament, combining strength and beauty, seems a better subject for art than the pallid subjects of "disenchanted days." Even Greece is to be spurned if it induces a longing for peace. In "The Islands," addressed to a lover and fellow-Hellenist, she notes that, like the Aegean islands, "beauty is set about/with wrecks of ships." The derelicts should remind the poet of the glorious dangers of art. If they cause him "to take fright of beauty,/terrible, torturous, isolated,/a barren rock," she doubts the validity of his Hellenism: "What is Greece if you draw back/from the terror/and cold splendour of song/and its bleak sacrifice?"

A more charming view of the life of a poet is given in "Heliodora" and "Nossis." "Heliodora"—based upon two epigrams by Meleager in *The Greek Anthology*—conveys the joyfulness of two poets' comradeship. The reader may imagine H. D. and Aldington in the guise of Meleager and the speaker. She writes: "He and I sought together,/over the spattered table,/rhymes and flowers,/ gifts for a name." Through the night, the two poets drink wine and vie at creating floral epithets for the girl Heliodora. As dawn appears, Meleager's epigram ends their affectionate competition, and the speaker acknowledges his triumph: "there will never be a poet/in all the centuries after this,/who will dare write,/after my friend's verse,/'a girl's mouth/is a lily kissed.'"

Love Desired and Feared

The intensity of the poems about nature and poetry is matched by those about love. However, the love poems express an ambiguity that is not present in H. D.'s handling of other topics. Toward nature and poetry, a single view is presented; she recognizes the difficulty of facing the violence of nature and of bearing the yoke of poetry, but she never wavers in her determination to do so. She prays for strength to persist in a cause that she never doubts. About love, she is not so single-minded. She sees the body and the spirit as conflicting: physical love is a threat to the spirit. Sensual passion is felt keenly, but she fears surrendering her self-autonomy. She is mindful, too, that love may not be reciprocated or, if reciprocated, may be lost. The relationship of love to art also worries her. Because she is aware of the urgency of love, she is afraid that her poetry may suffer if she passes under love's dominion. Yet she knows that love is a perennial subject of art.

One of the most arresting of these poems is the lengthy love-lyric "Hymen," the title piece of her second volume. It is actually a stately verse tableau or verse ballet, complete with stage directions and suggestions for musical accompaniment. In substance it is an epithalamion that calls to mind a marriage procession depicted on a Grecian urn or a temple frieze. Girls and women at various stages of life offer songs and bouquets to the bride as she prepares for the wedding. Love himself appears, followed by boys singing his praises. The bride is a "veiled symbolic figure . . . her head is swathed in folds of diaphanous white through which the features are visible, like the veiled Tanagra." Her quiescence suggests the submission of mankind to the approach of love. The emotions attending this climactic event are expressed by the choruses—all in the dignified manner of a religious ceremony.

First, sixteen matrons from the temple of Hera move before a curtain—"a dark purple hung between Ionic columns." Experienced in marriage, they chant their wish that, beyond the ecstasy of the nuptial season, "may one gift last"—presumably love itself. They are followed by attendants—four small girls. In the sweetness of their childhood, they have gathered choice crocus petals for the bride. Four older children carrying sprays of winter roses sing plaintively of the loss of their playmate. They know that she is entering a new life—"Never more/Shall we find you bright/In the snow and wind./. . . Like a light out of our heart,/ You are gone." Four "wood-maidens of Artemis," representing youth and spring, blithely sing of the loveliness of nature as they place hyacinth sprays about the bridal door. They seem unmindful of the solemnity of the event as they eagerly strew the chamber with flowers.

A chorus of bridal maidens next appears, surrounding the silent, veiled figure of the bride. They praise the beauty of her wedding garments and give their assurance that the bride herself is equally beautiful and is ready for the wedding: "For we know underneath/All the wanness,/All the heat/(In her blanched face)/Of desire/Is caught in her eyes as fire/In the dark center leaf/Of the white Syrian iris." They are followed by four young matrons who present bay blossoms whose hue, they promise, resembles the way her "fair breasts will shine/With the faint shadow above." Young women then arrive carrying linen for the bridal couch.

At last, Love appears—a tall youth, "a flame, an exaggerated symbol; the hair a flame; the wings, deep red or purple." He pauses just outside the bride's door with his gift, a tuft of black-purple cyclamen. His song—sensuous yet decorous—metaphorically describes a conjugal union:

There with his honey-seeking lips
The bee clings close and warmly sips,
And seeks with honey-thighs to sway
And drink the very flower away.

(Ah, stern the petals drawing back;
Ah rare, ah virginal her breath!)
Crimson, with honey-seeking lips,
The sun lies hot across his back,

The gold is flecked across his wings.
Quivering he sways and quivering clings
(Ah, rare her shoulders drawing back!)
One moment, then the plunderer slips
Between the purple flower-lips.

As Love leaves the stage, a band of boys gathers up the wreaths and petals. Then they raise hymeneal torches above their heads and sing of love's overwhelming mastery: "Where love is come/(Ah, love is come indeed!)/Our limbs are numb/Before his fiery need;/With all their glad/Rapture of speech unsaid,/Before his fiery lips/Our lips are mute and dumb." When the song ends, "the torches flicker out and the figures are no longer distinguishable in the darkness."

"Leda" is a briefer and deservedly more widely known poem about acquiescence to love. An exquisite lyric, it describes the meeting of the swan-god and Leda, here metamorphosed into a day-lily. Details of the swan's body, the sunset, and their encounter among the reeds "where tide and river meet" create an atmosphere of natural loveliness that makes the sensuous union of the couple seem idyllic—a pattern for mortal lovers:

> where the low sedge is thick,
> the gold day-lily
> outspreads and rests
> beneath soft fluttering
> of red swan wings
> and the warm quivering
> of the red swan's breast.

To this description, the poet adds only a single comment: "Ah kingly kiss—/no more regret/nor old deep memories/to mar the bliss."

A melancholy note about love is introduced in "Fragment Forty." Occasioned by the fragment by Sappho, "Love . . . bittersweet," this poem declares the mutability of love. Because the nature of Eros is fickle, it may even be a blessing to be free of his distressing presence. Moreover, the poet bravely asserts that, for the joy of love to be experienced, a human lover is not needed because a larger, cosmic love always surrounds us. Yet, she admits, to be able to sing of this spiritual love, ordinary "love must first shatter us."

Another verse from Sappho, "I know not what to do:/my mind is divided," is extended in "Fragment Thirty-Six" to express the tension between love and art. The poet, lying beside her sleeping lover, is torn between artistry and amorous desire. Her mind struggles like "two white wrestlers/standing for a match,/ready to turn and clutch/yet never shake muscle nor nerve nor tendon."

Should she interrupt her lover's rest—"Is love's gift best?"—or continue listening to "sound surging upon sound?" She reflects that, if love were lost, she could take no rapture from song; yet song must not be slighted. She cannot know how long the poetic impulse may last, nor can she know how her lover would react to being awakened. She fears to "press lips to flesh/that shudders not nor breaks." The simultaneous experience of love and art seems impossible, yet anything less seems unendurable.

The conflict of love and self-fulfillment is the subject of "Toward the Piraeus." The opening is a prayer to the ancient Greeks to destroy the "puny, passionless, weak" men of our time. Merely a single Grecian mantle would frighten "men, craven and weak." It is then disclosed that the poet has a Greek-like lover whose imperiousness threatens their relationship. "You would have broken my wings," she complains. His will would have enslaved her; yet "the very fact that you saw,/sheltered me, claimed me,/ set me apart from the rest." Realizing her special dignity, she is now bound to defend herself against spiritual annihilation. Even love must be resisted if it threatens her autonomy. She feels like the Pythoness in the temple of Apollo who must resist all distractions from the fulfillment of her destiny. Were she a boy, she might be her lover's friend; but, as a woman, she must reject him. The pathos of her situation is that she must oppose a man whose power sets him apart from "the puny race that crawls and quibbles and lisps." She must protect her selfhood from the one who has made her aware of it. She declares stoically:

> It was not chastity that made me wild, but fear
> that my weapon, tempered in different heat,
> was over-matched by yours, and your hand
> skilled to yield death-blows, might break
>
> With the slightest turn—no ill will meant—
> my own lesser, yet still somewhat fine-wrought,
> fiery-tempered, delicate, over-passionate steel.

The saddest of H. D.'s poems about love is "Fragment Forty-One"—based upon Sappho's ". . . thou flittest to Andromeda." The poet protests that she has neither scorned nor been scorned by love:

> I too have followed
> her path.
> I too have bent at her feet.

I too have wakened to pluck
amaranth in the straight shaft,
amaranth purple in the cup,
scorched at the edge to white.

She utters this protest for the most pitiable of reasons: she has been rejected by a lover who accuses her of frigidity. She must not only bear the torment of unrequited love—"my flesh so scorched and rent,/shattered, cut apart,/slashed open"—but defend herself from the charge of coldness. She insists to Aphrodite, "I was not asleep," "I was not unaware," "I was not blind," "I was not indifferent," "I was not dull and dead." She wishes to assure the goddess that she is grateful for past blessings and that even now she is not hostile toward love: "Lady of all beauty,/I give you this:/say I have offered small sacrifice,/say I am unworthy your touch,/but say not:/'she turned to some cold, calm god,/silent, pitiful, in preference.'" To prove her fidelity to Aphrodite, she is prepared to offer a gift to the goddess that "no one has dared to speak"—a gift made not in return for favors granted but despite their being withheld. She presents her loss of love as a tribute to the deity from whom all love springs:

I offer more than the lad
singing at your steps,
praise of himself,
his mirror his friend's face,
more than any girl,
I offer you this:
(grant only strength
that I withdraw not my gift,)
I give you my praise and this:
the love of my lover
for his mistress.

The bleak mood of "Fragment Sixty-Eight" is caused by the same unhappiness. H. D. uses Sappho's fragment ". . . even in the house of Hades" to express her wish to die. She tells her soldier-lover, "I envy you your chance of death." Having already been slain both by love and by having her love rejected, she would welcome her actual death: "What can death mar in me/that you have not?/. . . What can death send me/that you have not?" Yet, as in "Fragment Forty-One," she insists that she is not bitter, that to be immolated for love is a privilege:

Could I have known?
nay, spare pity,
though I break,
crushed under the goddess' hate,
though I fall beaten at last,
so high have I thrust my glance
up into her presence.

Do not pity me, spare that,
but how I envy you
your chance of death.

The failure of love is also undoubtedly reflected in two poems expressing a desire for relief from emotional turmoil—"Cuckoo Song" and "Lethe." "Cuckoo Song" celebrates the song of a gentle bird. His call does not summon the listener to passion and ecstasy; instead, it soothes and stills "the throbbing of our brain." The poet fancies that Calypso must have heard this call "across the gathering drift/of burning cedar-wood/. . ./when all her hope was dead." In "Lethe" this mood of hopelessness beyond grief yields to a willing anticipation of death. The appeal of death is that it will bring desire and disappointment to an end:

Nor word nor touch nor sight
Of lover, you
Shall long through the night but for this:
The roll of the full tide to cover you
Without question,
Without kiss.

Ancient Greece

Collected Poems also includes two poems about Greece: "Helen" and "Egypt." "Helen"—one of H. D.'s most admired lyrics—is concerned with man's fear of beauty because of the trouble it brings. Specifically, she fancies the attitude of the Greeks toward "God's daughter, born of love." They are irresistibly drawn toward her; yet they hate her for having occasioned the Trojan War. They would feel free to love her only if she were dead. Until then, "All Greece hates/the still eyes in the white face,/the lustre as of olives/ where she stands,/and the white hands."

In "Egypt," she imagines the attitude of an ancient Greek toward the older culture. She acknowledges the power of Egypt to debilitate the mind and the will. The implication is that the Egyptians' preoccupation with eternity included an undue emphasis upon dreams and reveries:

> Egypt had cheated us,
> for Egypt took
> through guile and craft
> our treasure and our hope,
> Egypt had maimed us,
> offered dream for life,
> an opiate for a kiss,
> and death for both.

She argues, "Egypt we loved, though hate/should have withheld our touch." Yet, she admits, by some "perverse fate," knowledge gained from Egypt has not reduced Greece to "trance,/shadow, fore-doom of death" but to "passionate grave thought,/belief enhanced,/ritual returned and magic." Egypt has nourished Greek thought from deeper springs than run on native soil; it has, indeed, brought about a "Hellas re-born from death." Significantly, H. D.'s last major work is the book-length poem *Helen in Egypt*; in it, the themes of these two early poems are richly developed.

III *Dramatic Monologues*

The remaining group in the collection consists of dramatic monologues, which introduce no new themes but reinforce those already discussed by ascribing them to ancient Greek personages —mythic, legendary, and fictitious. In the case of well-established figures like Circe, Cassandra, and Eurydice, the monologues blend traditional attitudes and H. D.'s personal views. It is indicative of H. D.'s skill that she violates neither her own views nor tradition. The reader might not imagine Phaedra exactly as H. D. does, but he should not find it difficult to do so.

Three are about art: "Pygmalion," "Orion Dead," and "Charioteer." Pygmalion ponders the central question of the creative imagination: what is the relationship between the artist's talent and gratuitous inspiration? "Have I made this fire from myself?/ or is this arrogance?/is this fire a god/that seeks me in the dark?" Orion the hunter observes that, since he has been "poisoned with rage of song," he has lost his interest in the chase: "I once pierced the flesh/of the wild deer,/now I am afraid to touch/the blue and the gold-veined hyacinths." "Charioteer" is dull: a sculptor's description of a chariot race in which his brother is a contestant. The brother wins, and the sculptor plans to make a statue of him as a tribute to the gods.

A few poems are occasional. In "Hermonax," a humble fisherman offers a gift to the sea gods in thanks for his safe return. In "At Eleusis," the speaker is "a mortal set in the goddess' place" at the Eleusinian mysteries. She watches the initiates trying to purge themselves of guilt by honestly admitting their faults. Some succeed; others find the ordeal unbearable. In "After Troy," a Trojan survivor of the war suggests that the Greeks have been victorious because they do not experience the sweet domination of Aphrodite.

The best poem in this miscellaneous group is "The Look-Out." The protagonist is Lynceus, the lookout on the *Argo*. He is aware that the rowers envy him his job, thinking it easier than theirs: "I hear:/. . ./'let Lynceus have my part,/let me rest like Lynceus.'" He protests that the men fail to understand that physical toil is easier than his task of guiding the ship through perilous waters. They do not know "what strange terror lurks in the sea-depth." Lynceus would gladly exchange his troubled inactivity for their sore muscles.

But Lynceus,
though they cannot guess
the hurt, though they do not thank
the oars for the dead peace
of heart and brain worn out,
you must wait,
alert, alert, alert.

The remaining sixteen dramatic monologues are about love. As one would expect, almost all concern the amorous conflicts of women—especially unrequited desire, disappointment, rivalry, misgivings, and betrayal. The most affirmative are "Evadne" and "Centaur Song." In them the subject is the joy of love. Both present non-human beings as ideal lovers. Evadne sings of the ecstasy of being loved by Apollo:

His hair was crisp to my mouth
as the flower of the crocus,
across my cheek,
cool as the silver cress
on Erotos bank;
between my chin and throat
his mouth slipped over and over.

"Centaur Song" also celebrates a perfect love. Since the lover is half-animal, H. D. is able to make literal use of imagery from nature. The setting actually consists of flowers, trees, and reeds: "Now that the day is done,/now that the night creeps soft/and dims the chestnut clusters'/radiant spike of flower,/O sweet, till dawn/break through the branches/of our orchard garden,/rest in this shelter/of the osier-wood and thorn."

Other monologues recount less happy relationships. In "Simaetha," a girl has been offended by her lover. She wonders if, when he returns to her, she will be as ardent as before or will be "white as ash bled of heat,/white as hail blazing in sheet-lightning,/white as forked lightning/rending the sleet." Penelope, in "At Ithaca," is beset by "weary thoughts" that impel her to accept one of her suitors. Fortunately, Athena strengthens her resolution to be loyal to Odysseus. In "Eurydice," the unlucky bride reproaches Orpheus for dooming her to remain in Hades by looking back at her as they climb earthward. She calls him arrogant and ruthless for denying her the chance to enjoy the colors of earth. Yet she claims that in one respect her fate is better than his: she shines beside the blackness of Hades; he is paled by the brightness of earth. She adds that as long as she has her own "spirit for light" she is not lost. "Circe" tells of the enchantress' grief at losing Olysseus: all her triumphs over lesser men seem paltry in the face of her failure to enslave him. "Demeter" and "Thetis" are rather obscure expressions of the troubles of goddesses. Demeter seems resentful that other goddesses have been preferred before her, and Thetis expresses herself more like Achilles' lover than his mother. In "Lais," an aging beauty offers her mirror to Aphrodite because she no longer sees in it the loveliness "that laughed exultant/tyrannizing Greece."

Love conflicts with other interests in "Telesila" and "Cassandra." The poet Telesila reflects upon her decision to renounce love poetry in order to defend Argos against Sparta. She is uneasy and even wishes that love had so dominated her that she could have turned her back entirely upon patriotism. However, she had no choice: Ares placed her under his power. Nevertheless, she doubts the value of her sacrifice. "Cassandra" is a more moving poem, perhaps because H. D. felt its conflict more intimately. The prophetess, described as if she were also a poet, beseeches Hymen either to satisfy her longing for love or to allow her to live completely in the visionary world of the seer. She cannot endure the agony of being shifted from one realm to the other: "speak, nameless, power and might;/when will you leave me quite?/when will you break my wings/or leave them utterly free/to scale heaven endlessly?" Without love she feels lonely, especially since her reputation as a prophet causes people to fear her—"if I but pass they fall/back, frantically." She prays: "may Love not lie beside me/till his heat/burn me to ash?"

Particularly praiseworthy are four monologues based on the Phaedra-Hippolytus tale: "Hippolytus Temporizes," "Phaedra," "She Contrasts with Herself Hippolyta," and "She Rebukes Hippolyta." These poems are H. D.'s preliminary handling of a subject that she later treated in her verse-drama *Hippolytus Temporizes.* In the lyric of the same title, Hippolytus is in conflict over his pledge of chastity to Artemis. Each stanza begins with a declaration of loyalty to the goddess, but the remainder of the stanza is a parenthetical outpouring of desire for Phaedra. In the second stanza, he thinks:

(as, sweet, your eyes—
what God, invoked in Crete,
gave them the gift to part
as the Sidonian myrtle-flower
suddenly, wide and swart,
then swiftly,
the eye-lids having provoked our hearts—
as suddenly beat and close.)

"Phaedra" presents the love-stricken queen in a sympathetic light. She feels herself being irresistibly drawn toward Hippolytus. In the past, she has been strong-willed; now her will is "caught in a force, a power,/passionless, not its own." She implores the gods of her native Crete:

> *Grant to my soul*
> *the body that it wore,*
> *trained to your thought,*
> *that kept and held your power,*
> *as the petal of black poppy,*
> *the opiate of the flower.*

She realizes that her prayer is powerless, that she is helpless: "The poppy that my heart was,/formed to bind all mortals,/made to strike and gather hearts/like flame upon an altar,/fades and shrinks, a red leaf/drenched and torn in the cold rain."

In "She Contrasts with Herself Hippolyta," Phaedra wonders about Hippolytus' mother, the Amazon. She decides that a child as cold to love as Hippolytus must have been born of a loveless union—"Theseus sought Hippolyta;/she yielded not nor broke,/sword upon stone,/from the clash leapt a spark,/Hippolytus, born of hate." She then wonders if Hippolyta could have failed to love her child. Phaedra feels that she herself could not be so cold-hearted. She decides, at any rate, that Hippolyta must have dedicated the child to the virgin huntress Artemis and thus occasioned Hippolytus' resistance to love.

"Was she so chaste?" asks Phaedra in "She Rebukes Hippolyta." She fancies that Hippolyta saw a perfect lover figured in the hills and fields:

> the broken ridge of the hills
> was the line of a lover's shoulder,
> his arm-turn, the path to the hills,
> the sudden leap and swift thunder
> of mountain boulders, his laugh.

Thus, when the magnificent Theseus charged upon her, Hippolyta must have thought him the nature-god of her dreams and willingly yielded herself to him. Thus:

> she, the chaste,
> was betrayed by the glint
> of light on the hills,
> the granite splinter of rocks,
> the touch of the stone
> where heat melts
> toward the shadow-side of the rocks.

IV *Conclusion*

These poems demonstrate H. D.'s characteristic poetic mode: the expression in free verse of images drawn from nature. The refinements of her style have been aptly described by Babette Deutsch: "H. D.'s rhythms are almost the rhythms of speech, but speech at its most passionate, restrained by the very emotion with which it is charged. The lines are short, often monosyllabic, yet heavy with emphasis. Rhyme is used sparingly and not always effectively, but only in the longer poems and the verse dramas [written later than *Collected Poems*] are the insistent repetitions felt as a flaw. Elsewhere, the frequent spondees, the recurrence of certain phrases, the parallelism of others, produce an effect of symmetry."[11]

H. D.'s outlook is marked by her longing for an intense realization of nature, art, and love; she detests complacency and mediocrity. Scorning a life of comfortable dilettantism, she wants dangerous and rare psychic experiences—comparable to scaling Himalayan peaks and exploring coral reefs. Seeking extreme goals requires absolute commitment and separates her from ordinary society. To H. D., the difficulty of her quest is a warrant of its value. Experiencing nature's untamed vitality, the harmony of art, and the ecstasy of love are satisfactions worth every sacrifice. She gladly renounces the attractions sought by most people; what tortures her is the elusiveness of what she seeks, especially since her aims tend to conflict with each other. Love wars with poetry, and poetry with nature; yet she remains steadfast in pursuit of them all.

These themes are expressed in poems that are limited but compelling. Their restricted range—a counterpart of their intensity—has often been recognized. Amy Lowell wrote candidly: "This is a narrow art, it has no scope, it neither digs deeply nor spreads widely. Not that it is superficial; it is quite the reverse. But merely that 'there are more things in Heaven and Earth' than such poetry takes cognizance of."[12] This limitation results not only from H. D.'s avoidance of contemporary details and issues but also from the selectivity of her classicism. Many aspects of ancient Greek life are missing in H. D.'s highly personal view.

The spirit of these poems bespeaks an ardent temperament in pursuit of transcendental satisfaction. On such terms, H. D.'s quest seems sure to fail; yet she makes no allowance for failure. Her repugnance for any condition short of the absolute is as strong as her yearning for fulfillment. In her relationship with nature, art, and love, she wishes to experience a sacredness usually associated with religious worship: nature is to be God's arena; art, God's inspiration; and love, God's incarnation. Actually, she seems to enjoy some measure of success only with nature; her hope for the attainment of inspired artistry is set toward the future, and her desire for love has been disappointed. Visions of ecstatic union with gods are matched by admissions of betrayal by men.

CHAPTER 3

Prose Fiction

PALIMPSEST (1926),[1] *Hedylus* (1928),[2] and *Bid Me to Live* (1960)[3] are H. D.'s principal works of fiction. All three works are harmonious in theme and technique, even though *Bid Me to Live* was not published until 1960, more than thirty years after the others. This last novel particularly resembles two of the three sections of *Palimpsest*—"Murex" and "Secret Name." Why so many years passed before *Bid Me to Live* was published is not known, but the personal nature of the material may have been partly responsible. Although it springs from the same psychological experiences that are reflected in *Hedylus* and *Palimpsest*, it contains the most intimate episodes of the three and presents them in a virtually undisguised manner.

The settings of these works vary from ancient Greece and Rome to modern England and Egypt. However, one question—akin to the major theme of *Collected Poems*—dominates them all: how is a sensitive woman to cope with the world? By sensitivity, H. D. means a responsiveness to nature, art, and beauty. Ultimately, she means a desire for a mystical experience: for the realization of absolute beauty and love. Opposing this quest is the world—violent, vulgar, and trivial. The "world" is everything that hampers the cultivation of the spirit; yet it is also the arena within which the spirit must prevail.

In dramatizing the conflict of the world and the spirit, H. D. addresses herself to several more specific problems. First, there is the difficulty of achieving selfhood. She realizes that each person inherits physical and psychological traits that seem to be both part of himself and distinguishable from himself. Where, she wonders, in this network does the self reside, if it can be said to exist at all? She also considers the accidents of time and place. In these novels, the time varies from ancient to modern; the settings shift from Rome, to England, to Samos, to Egypt;

and conditions change from war to peace. H. D. is sensitive to the fortuitous elements in every person's life; yet she probes these layers of accidental differences in search of a substratum of universality. Her interest in ancient myths is involved in her quest for the relevance of mythic patterns in all ages.

She also explores the relationship between love and art. The imperious claim of each is willingly acknowledged, but their mutual antagonism is also recognized. Love, by placing self-autonomy in jeopardy, threatens the alert passivity required by art. Conversely, art is a solitary commitment, which, by isolating the artist from others, is a deterrent to love. H. D. sees that art may be a refuge from life, but she believes that in such a case art as well as love is doomed. Generally, she presents love and art as aspects of each other, but she emphasizes the difficulty of achieving their harmony. She also has an ambiguous attitude toward nature. She cherishes it for its own sake and as a stimulant to art, but she also sees it as an obstacle to culture and love. Finally, all of these problems are considered from a woman's point of view. They are, of course, the basic problems of mankind; but H. D. is sensitive to the way they are experienced by women.

The same literary technique is used throughout the three books. Each story is told in the third person by a narrator who frequently merges with the protagonist. The result is a combination of impersonal and stream-of-consciousness narration. Theoretically, this blend offers the reader both the immediacy of the stream-of-consciousness and the detachment of an objective narrator. H. D. often achieves this two-sided effect, but sometimes the transition from one to the other is awkward. The general tone is colloquial—the speech of a well-bred, nervous woman (only in *Hedylus* is the narrator ever closely identified with a male character). There is seldom any direct presentation of action; events are implied and gradually confirmed through the narrator's reflections.

The result is a drama of the inner life, intense with consciousness and vivid with metaphor. Ordinary circumstances are important principally as magnets for personal associations; happenings glow with subjective significance. This type of fiction tends toward the condition of a Symbolist poem—details recognizable at the outset lose their conventional value, drift uncertainly for a time in the reader's consciousness, and then, if the writing is successful, take on a superior value as archetypes of human experience. Starting with patient perplexity, the reader is to be drawn into a powerful, vicarious experience.

I Palimpsest

Palimpsest, dedicated to H. D.'s friend Bryher, has a subtitle that both defines this unusual word and suggests the structure of the book: "a palimpsest, i. e. a parchment from which one writing has been erased to make room for another." H. D.'s supposed parchment contains three tales of about equal length: "Hipparchia," "Murex," and "Secret Name." The title page states that "Hipparchia" is set in "War Rome" about 75 B.C., "Murex" in "War and post-war London" from 1916 to 1926, and "Secret Name" in "Excavator's Egypt" about 1925.

The layers of text on a palimpsest—should it be possible to read any but the topmost—bear no necessary relation to each other. They were superimposed because of the high cost of parchment, not from a desire to create literary puzzles. H. D.'s *Palimpsest* is another matter: it is not a relic of the past but a deliberate composition. Even though the title does not commit H. D. to establishing a kinship among the parts, the reader expects her to do so.

Such, in fact, is the case. The three sections express similar interests, even though each section has a different setting and plot. Either read consecutively or encountered apart from each other, they are easily recognized as the expression of the same author. This homogeneity is true of H. D.'s other novels as well. *Hedylus* and *Bid Me to Live* might be joined to *Palimpsest* with no loss of harmony.

"Hipparchia"

"Hipparchia," the first section, is an elaborate fiction based upon a verse from the poem "Hipparchia" by Antipater of Sidon. H. D. uses this verse as an epigraph: "I cast my lot with cynics, not with women seated at the distaff." In this respect, "Hipparchia" resembles the lyrics in *Collected Poems* that are based upon single verses by Sappho.

The setting is given as "War Rome—(circa 75 B.C.)"; the war is a Roman campaign in Greece against Mithridates. H. D. emphasizes that Rome at that time was strongly influenced by Greek culture. Greece was a conquered land, but its people possessed a civilization that the Romans recognized as superior to their own—imperial power excepted. The principal characters react to one another chiefly in terms of the opposition between force and culture; their lives illustrate the struggle of the human spirit against all forms of coercion.

Hipparchia is a young woman who has been brought to Rome from Corinth—a displaced person of the war. She is a poet and a translator from Greek to Latin. Her father is the Cynic philosopher Crates; her mother is the Hipparchia referred to in the epigraph. Following the fall of Corinth, Crates went into exile in order to continue his search for mystical fulfillment; his wife went with him, casting her lot "with cynics, not with women seated at the distaff." To their daughter Hipparchia, Crates is a shadowy figure whose behavior seems strange and unattractive. She wonders how her mother could abandon an elegant life in order to accompany her husband into exile. To her, they seem to have rejected both nature and culture for the sake of some transcendental will-o'-the-wisp.

When her parents left, Hipparchia remained in Corinth with Philip, a young half-uncle whom she admired greatly. He was a botanist, and often he took Hipparchia with him in search of specimens. On one of their excursions, they unwittingly approached the Roman line of fortification, and Philip was fatally wounded by a sentinel. After Philip's death, Hipparchia went to Rome.

As the story opens, Hipparchia is the mistress of Marius Decius, an officer in the Roman army. To Marius, she is "the somewhat exotic high-strung girl that he had singled out from the usual exuberant crowd at the house of his brother-in-law" (10-11). They have not been getting along well. Hipparchia complains to him that, "when one has slept perhaps on a rough estimate, one hundred and fifty times with one man, it is, can you not see, somewhat of a shock, at the end, to find it has not been a man at all, merely a rather bulbous vegetable" (14). He retorts, "I have just discovered that . . . I slept not with a woman but a phantom" (14).

The source of their trouble is Hipparchia's contempt for the Romans. She considers herself a Corinthian, a survivor of a high civilization that has been overcome by a boorish military power. The lines of Antipater of Sidon's dirge for Corinth haunt her memory:

> Where Corinth, charm incarnate, are your shrines?
> your citadel, your towered wall, your line
> of noble women? Your ancient treasure?
> and that ten-thousand of your people lost?
>
> War wreaked on you his hideous ravishment,
> we, we alone, Neriads inviolate,
> remain to weep, with the sea gulls to chant,
> Corinth is lost, Corinth is desolate.

She clings to the belief that the conqueror will be overcome by his victim—that the Hellenic spirit will prevail over the power of Rome. "Romans are wine pressers," she often thinks. "Romans were too crude. Could they not see that the very plunder they had saved from Corinth would undo them? . . . Greek must rule. Not Rome only but the world" (103).

Although Hipparchia accuses Marius of typical Roman vulgarity, he does not deserve such censure. His choice of so dreamy a girl as Hipparchia indicates an unconventional taste. In fact, his fellow officers think that he is not earthy enough for success in the army. His ideal is to combine spirituality and physical passion. Hipparchia promised both but he has found her lacking in passion. He sees her as the Greek spirit incarnate, but a spirit that has grown morbid and disembodied through overcultivation and political defeat. "We fight, fighting Greeks, some supernatural Spirit," he remarks to another officer (27); and for him Hipparchia is this spirit, both appealing and frightening. "She was something come to plague, to destroy. It was for this that she had condescended" (12). The ambivalence of his attitude is exhibited in his response to their love-making. He resents her passivity: "Plunge dagger into a gold lily. What more was she, had she in her most intimate encounters given him?" (7). Yet, in possessing her, "he breathed in some relic of a vanished and a vanquished loveliness" (39). Uncertain of his mastery, he longed "to bring to the thin, rather colourless lips the stark agonizing cry for pity that would finally prove Rome conqueror" (17).

Unwilling to endure the strain of their relationship, Marius leaves Hipparchia and becomes the lover of Olivia, a voluptuous Sicilian who presents no cultural and spiritual complications:

"To look at Olivia gave him spiritual release. She was so simply, so whole-heartedly a woman" (32). However, Hipparchia's nature resembles a part of his own, and a short time later, while recovering from a battle wound, he explains to her in a letter why he has left her and why he continues to need her:

> I think the thing I hated most in Hipparchia was her curious sublimating quality. She thought this or no. Therefore by some witchcraft of intellectualisation we who loved her, were forced by a sort of suggestive hypnosis to become, in some subtle manner, somewhat of the thing, she, in her high mind, saw fit to see us. Olivia is just Olivia. . . . Then finally when boredom had a little cleansed the citadel that is the somewhat unreliable soul of your Marius, I felt creeping like some insinuating wraith, or mist, the old glamour, the old insatiety, a disease, a mental unsteadiness, a thing that inexplicably lifts me out of my confining heavy members. I call it just Hipparchia. (61-62)

Unfortunately, he later disavows this declaration as merely a symptom of his anxiety about death. Once recovered, he returns to Olivia; soon afterward their wedding plans are announced.

Hipparchia, abandoned by her "bulbous vegetable," becomes the mistress of Quintus Verrus, a Roman of a different stamp altogether. He is a scholar who maintains a handsome villa at Capua. At first, Hipparchia finds his meticulous and quiet manner a relief from Marius' soldierly vigor. Their love-making is described as a gentle, though chilly, encounter: "There had been no striving. So Artemis must, she felt, have caught between long arms the form of young Endymion. Snow (in her apprehension) caught and tangled in the wisps of her pollen-dusted hair. . . . Snow permeating, penetrating, (no thrusting, counter-parrying of soldiers at sword-play) till snow and snow were one, a new Danae with more frail god-embodiment" (53). Before long, however, she recognizes that Verrus is a dilettante "marred by sloth, by singular indifference. This was (to her) wickedness" (71). Despite his predilection for Egyptian culture—with which he opposes her loyalty to Greek ideals—she finds him spiritually barren and soon leaves him.

After being disappointed by both her manly and her dispassionate lovers, Hipparchia realizes that her strongest desire is for beauty. In order to be true to this pursuit, she resolves to be wary of personal relationships. She is particularly determined to avoid sexual affairs: "She wanted intimacy without intercourse." Platonic friendship would be a boon, of course, "but," she admits sadly, "who offers comradeship without passion?" (92-93). She decides to devote herself to the solitary task of completing a book on plants begun by her uncle Philip. It is to be more than a scientific treatise: a combination of natural history, myth, and literature—"Why the Bacchus of Ariadne chose the purple ivy, why the Hera of Argos favoured heliochrysos" (98). She hopes to create a work that will show the Romans the cultural superiority of Greece.

To carry out her plan, she moves to Tusculum; and, as a sign that her old life has ended, she discards her finery. In so doing, she is able for the first time to understand her mother's renunciation of luxury. She works intensely at her task. Since it is a continuation of her beloved Philip's work, she is spurred by a sense of his presence: "Philip was her passion, her intellect, her mind which none had broken. . . . This is true marriage. Philip shows me true enlightenment" (102). "Philip said better, better, better, work, work, work. . . . Philip was a sword, Philip was her mind" (111).

After driving herself relentlessly for a time, she becomes ill and unfit for a strict regimen of isolation and work. Her plan for self-realization is balked. Her nerves buckle; her creative energy is exhausted, and she sinks into a melancholy hysteria. The entire enterprise of writing seems pointless: "Of what use was poetry and inspiration? . . . Of what use was intellect?" (114). "She was through with writing. . . . Song was futile against a bird note that cut with insistent anguish the very veils of winter" (119). Her spirit is so diminished that she considers returning to Verrus. Feeling drained of life, she considers herself a fit companion for the pallid dilettante.

She is spared this humiliation by a turn of fortune. A visitor calls and, despite being turned away, keeps returning until Hipparchia consents to see her. Contrary to Hipparchia's fear that the caller is some vulgar person in search of a tutor, it is a shy young girl: "My name is Julia Cornelia Augusta. I am the daughter of Enneus Lauditer. My father and I are both interested in your manuscripts" (125). Momentarily, Hipparchia has the illusion that Julia is Moero, the exquisite Greek lyricist whose poems she has been trying to translate. Slowly she realizes that she is not suffering from a hallucination but is being offered a new life. Julia's father is a wealthy traveler who is about to visit Greece and Alexandria, for he "collects everything that is Greek" (129). Julia already admires Hipparchia's writing, having learned all her translations by heart. Both father and daughter wish Hipparchia to accompany them on their journey, for she has helped them to love Greece. When Hipparchia protests that Greece is a conquered land, Julia replies that Greece is an invincible spirit. Hearing her own belief echoed so well, Hipparchia exclaims joyfully: "Someone said *Greece is a spirit. Greece is not lost.* I will come with you" (131). At this point the story ends.

At a stroke, Hipparchia's problems seem to be settled. She has found an admiring woman friend—probably the best way to satisfy her wish for "intimacy without intercourse." Also, since Julia's father is rich, Hipparchia's finery may soon be restored. She has been rescued from both the servitude of a mistress and the morbidity of isolation. Moreover, her benefactors look upon her as a living representative of the culture they have come to love. As Roman converts to Hellenism, they confirm Hipparchia's hope for the ultimate triumph of Greece. With them, she can look forward to leisure for her translations and encouragement to produce her finest work.

Of course, since the narration ends before Hipparchia gets to know her new friends, her future remains problematical. Dependence upon the admiration of a young girl and her wealthy father may create difficulties, but for the moment Hipparchia is hopeful. After finding men either physically or intellectually dissatisfying, and solitude unbearable, she gladly accepts their offer. The reader may be surprised at so sudden and neat a solution; he may even fear that at best the arrangement is too snug for credibility or for Hipparchia's continued spiritual growth. However, H. D. does not even glance at these darker possibilities.

"Murex"

Although "Murex" is set in London, 1926, the principal character, Raymonde Ransome, closely resembles Hipparchia. Even more, she resembles H. D. herself. Like Hipparchia and H. D., Raymonde is a writer who has been the victim of love and war. Like H. D., she is an American poet who has lived through World War I in London and now divides the year between Switzerland and England. To carry the resemblance further, she publishes under a *nom de plume* (Ray Bart); she has been married to an English poet who served in the war, and she has lost a child by miscarriage and a husband by default.

The narrator records Raymonde's consciousness during an afternoon in her London flat. A telephone caller asks if Raymonde will see a girl they both know. The girl comes to tea; after she leaves, Raymonde reflects upon the visit and writes a poem. The irony is that their brief chat transforms Raymonde's life. Unwittingly, the visitor forces her to face the most painful episodes of her past life.

The caller, Ermentrude (Ermy) Solomon, is an actress who became a war-widow at the age of eighteen. The expressed purpose of her visit is to get letters of introduction to people in Florence, Italy; but she really wants sympathy for her latest misfortune in love. She tells Raymonde that she and her boy friend Martin had been guests at the country home of Mavis Landour, an old friend of Raymonde's, and Mavis had seduced Martin. Unknown to Ermy, this news is traumatic to Raymonde because it reminds her of her own unhappy relationship with Mavis. Like Ermy, she has been a victim of Mavis' ruthlessness about love: ten years earlier Mavis had stolen Raymonde's husband Freddie.

She is particularly upset by Ermy's hostility toward Mavis because for years Raymonde has been trying to suppress this feeling. She has struggled to think as little as possible about the loss of her husband and, when thinking of it, to keep from blaming anyone. She senses that if she permits herself to indulge in self-pity and rancor over Mavis' behavior (Raymonde at the time had been hospitalized because of a miscarriage) she might be driven out of her mind. Instead, she has disciplined herself to repress any feeling that she has been a failure at love or a victim of injustice. She has lived in Switzerland most of each year and concentrated upon her writing. The beauty of Switzerland, free of any association with her past life, has permitted her to use her mind creatively. Now and then needing a change, she has visited London, but on terms that have preserved her peace of mind. She has avoided social engagements and, when she has accidentally met friends from the war years, she has pretended an indifference toward the past that has even deceived herself.

In London she finds it easy to view the past calmly. For her, the city is conducive to apathy: "London had one season. Spring, winter, summer, they were all blurred in an ineffable half-light. Raymonde found here that corresponding twilight of the spirit. . . . Raymonde loved her London for just this; that there was no pulse and dart of static right and wrong" (135-36). In this atmosphere she is able to believe that "tragedy . . . couldn't in England actually exist" (139). During this latest visit, she has urgently needed to use London as such a "twilight of the spirit," for memories of the war have been distressing her in Switzerland.

Ermy, the visitor, penetrates Raymonde's spiritual coma. She represents the war—her young husband was killed in it. Worse still, Ermy's defeat in love parallels Raymonde's: Mavis has deceived them both. Moreover, Ermy is not willing to resign herself to her misfortune. She is full of resentment and self-pity; she denounces Mavis and sees herself as an innocent victim. Hearing Ermy, Raymonde is no longer able to wear her mask of indifference but is compelled to face herself:

> Ermy (a highly refined surface) collected, concentrated, gave her back a self that she had so long let drift under drug and anodine of London. Ermy gave her not so much Ermy or Mavis as sheer Raymonde. Frighteningly, in avid clarity, Ermy gave her Raymonde and so clear did that Raymonde seem that again Raymonde turned (changing sides, changing now the angle of her observance with almost every heart-beat) against Raymonde. In a second, Raymonde didn't want so to contemplate undiluted Raymonde. (167)

The unwanted confrontation is made, and Raymonde discovers that the experiences she has refused to face consciously have remained fresh in her unconscious mind—"doors had opened, a whole realm had been revealed that had been there, it seemed, all the time" (197). Her repossession of the past then takes place rapidly: "Yes, Mavis had taken Freddie. Raymonde admitted this now clearly in her conscious mind for almost the first time in half a dozen years" (162); "for the first time in almost ten years Raymonde was thinking consciously of Freddie" (189).

Her effort to cope with these newly acknowledged painful memories is the subject of the remaining part of the narration. Ermy has left, and while the afternoon wanes, Raymonde faces her past. Not surprisingly, her reflections are fragmentary and discordant, but from their disorder several ways of accepting unhappiness occur to her. One—of considerable interest because it is virtually the only explicit reference to Christianity in H. D.'s early work—is to follow Christ's injunction to love one's enemy. When Raymonde admits to herself that Mavis stole her husband, she feels outraged: "Savonarola rose in Raymonde and Raymonde recognized in herself the suppressed religio-maniac. . . . Savonarola dominant in every Puritan, reactionary or otherwise woke within her" (187). This censorious impulse is calmed by remembering that behind Savonarola stands Christ. She tells herself: "Christ had been right; love those that persecute—that persecute you. Love Mavis. . . . The laws of Christ were written in flower petals, were cloud and fire. They permeated the temple of ancient Greece like blue incense. Thou shalt love—permeated the temples of the Nile where they had already written these things in vast scrolls" (223). However, she finds this command difficult to obey, especially in the case of Mavis, who, Raymonde believes, has violated equally basic laws of loyalty and friendship.

Raymonde wonders also if she might be liberated from the painfulness of her predicament by practicing spiritual detachment. She wishes to see personal events as inevitable. In this connection she thinks of a famous contemporary: "James Joyce was right. Inflexible laws were to be read in the meanest actions" (213). She is doubtless thinking of the recently published *Ulysses* in which the meanderings of Leopold Bloom and Stephen Dedalus assert themselves as paradigms of history and human nature. Correspondingly, she would like to see in the drama of Freddie, Mavis, and Raymonde the inevitability of a Greek tragedy.

Help in achieving this goal is available to Raymonde because she is a poet. To her, poetry means self-surrender to a creative impulse that recognizes universal archetypes in personal events. In a metaphor of the sea that explains the title of this section, Raymonde expresses her belief that art can penetrate human experience to its core of universality: "Life was one huge sea and flat on its surface, merging, mingling was the business of existence. Verses. That meant diving, deep, deep, deep—*Who fished the murex up*?" (226-37). In this connection, too, she refers to James Joyce as a fellow artist who was aware of the sacred character of their vocation: "Art was magic—but it had lost—had lost —its savour. Joyce was right. It had lost. Art was magic but it had lost. Must get back into art the magic it had had in Egypt, Greece even" (219).

As though to confirm her faith in art—and at the same time to show how much personal sacrifice it demands—Raymonde is impelled to write a poem about Mavis. Despite her fatigue and disinclination, an irresistible force overrides her personal will, transforming her from Raymonde into her literary *alter-ego* Ray Bart:

> A line came on and on, and in the now renewed porcelain white electric glare she tried (in spite of writing pad almost visibly palpitating with expectancy on the little table—she had pushed aside the tea-things) to fend it off. With the very pencil she held poised, she tried to fend off her recurrent metres for what did it matter—she was no judge, never had been a judge of Mavis. She judge Mavis? It was part of her pride, of her not quite diminished glory that she should not. *Now she may say that I adore her face.* One little poem was enough. The icy glamour of the thing she knew was Ray Bart's helmet closed above her. Above Raymonde's forehead (where she would have worn some slight and fragrant but soon withering little crown of field flowers) Ray Bart's helmet rested. The helmet of Ray Bart weighed heavy on her. (209)

Verses from this poem, interspersed throughout the remainder of this section, express resignation to Mavis' behavior and awe at the attractiveness of such a woman.

Raymonde also considers a negative way of dealing with her unhappiness: ignoring it by turning to other interests. "She must find other things, not stare and stare any longer into the crystal ball of her past, all the memories shut up in one small spherical surface, her own head, to be watched going round and round and round" (244). This method of coping with trouble is just a step away from Raymonde's former determination to lose consciousness of painful facts. However, she does not incline to this alternative. It represents merely a fleeting, futile wish that difficulties could be overcome so easily. Her emphasis is clearly upon the saving and hieratic power of poetry. Appropriately, therefore, the section is concluded by the final lines of her poem:

> O fair, O just
> see now I would prepare
> a silver crown
> a holy diadem,

no rust shall stain my sword,
it shall gleam gracious,
silver-white for her,
deadly intriguant,

poisonous, with power
I hated; see—I worship,
more, more, more—I love her
who has sent you to my door.

"Secret Name"

"Secret Name," the final section of *Palimpsest*, contains several elements already established in "Hipparchia" and "Murex." The protagonist, Helen Fairwood, resembles Raymonde Ransome in being an American in her thirties who has lived through World War I in London. Like Hipparchia, she is a Hellenophile, something of a scholar; and she becomes friendly with an admiring young woman who, in this case, is traveling with her mother, a wealthy American. Like Hipparchia, also, Helen is preoccupied with culture and self-realization. Like both Hipparchia and Raymonde, she has been disappointed in love with an army officer; she is slender and nervous, and she is subject to "psycho-hysterical visionary sensations" (266). With more humor than the other two women show, she reflects that she and her friend could, "save for the warm glow of some inner interplay of curiosity (of, put it at its real value, intellect) be taken for invalids, for thin, frayed bits of feminine wreckage" (327).

The new element in this section is Egypt, but even this innovation serves to link the ancient and modern settings of the earlier sections. The action takes place in Thebes and Karnak—H. D. offers a subtitle, "Excavator's Egypt"—around 1925. Helen Fairwood and her female friends the Thorpe-Whartons are staying at the Luxor Hotel while they visit the ancient monuments, particularly the recently opened tombs of King Tutankhamen and Queen Hatepshet. Helen is a research assistant to Bodge-Grafton, an Egyptologist who is on hand to determine if the recent archeological finds will require him to alter the final volume of his masterwork. Helen, a Graeco-Roman scholar herself, has published a "half dozen terrible little articles . . . terrible, intense, erudite and in their limited way, illuminating and terribly right" (269).

Helen is deeply moved by what seems to be her first visit to

Egypt. She is grateful for the opportunity to study a major area of the ancient world, but she also finds Egypt a threat to her cultural convictions and to her self-composure. She has been a Hellenist, committed to ideals that she associates with the "fine-etched strife, with thought, with Athens" (250). Standing before the sphinxes and tombs, she finds the Hellenic quest for the perfection of humankind challenged by a different outlook:

> In Greece . . . there was that strange insistence upon human achievement. One measured oneself by the tiny Niké temple, out-jutting on the Acropolis. . . . Here was magnificence of another order. The mere human frame was so dwarfed that subconsciously one was required . . . to wear some robe of blatant indifference, of humility, of disdain. Not of despair. . . . Of what use was ambition and achievement? Of what possible meaning that dart and pulse of steel, of measured light, that was the very apt and prevalent image of her thought? Of what use the chariot of the soul and the measuring and countermeasuring of self against self, the adequate giving to each self its due, the self of intellect, the self of the drift and dream of anodine, the intermediate self, that slender balancing pole that held the two together, joined the two, keeping them strictly separate. Here there was no need of measure, of self-scale, of flinging (as at Paestum as at Athens) oneself upward, stretched tiptoe to one's highest spiritual height, measuring oneself by the measure, so strictly subtle, of the gods. The Athenian made a god, strict and subtle against which a human soul could (by standing tip-toe) by making the greatest of physical and psychic effort, yet contrast himself. He was (to the god) a brother, dwarfed yet still a human relative. In Egypt there was this unassuming comfort. One measured oneself by new and as yet unpremeditated standards. (296-97)

In short, Egypt threatens her self-confidence. Whereas Greek culture has provided examples encouraging to her pursuit of truth and beauty, in Egypt "the sky gave her assurance that she, after all, was nothing" (300). The heavy atmosphere and the overwhelming dimensions of the monuments discourage her from intellectual effort. In this environment, the goal of even her most vaulting ambition seems puny. Her desire for self-cultivation is debilitated by the unlikelihood and insignificance of success.

Reacting to this unexpected development, Helen fears losing what she already possesses. She feels that her "hard-won, specific

Attic paradise" (251) is at stake; yet she also recognizes that her Hellenism has a limitation that she would like to overcome: "She wanted to dive deep, deep, courageously down into some unexploited region of the consciousness, into some common deep sea of knowledge and bring, triumphant, to the surface some treasure buried, lost, forgotten" (255). Egypt seems to be a portal to this "unexploited region of the consciousness," but in approaching it "she feared lest with cautious Attic brain, she might freeze at the moment of discovery" (251). She fears also that she may succumb irretrievably to this new element: "lest she herself should slide into it, be lost, her personality be lost sliding, drawn inward as some bright-winged tenuous insect drawn down and inward into the honey-dusted centre of some white, enormous flower" (290).

Egypt tempts Helen to surrender her individuality to passion. For her, Athens represents the victory of intelligence and self-control; Egypt encourages her to yield her will to physical and cosmic forces. In particular, Egypt arouses her desire for sexual experience. In the temples she sees "great fervid buds, not like the columns of the Greeks that hold in their straight fair line a sort of challenge, not an appeal so much as a command to the intellect to soar up and up. These bulbous buds, enormous, pregnant, seemed endowed after these four thousand years with some inner life; to still hold that possibility of sudden bloom-burst" (303). Egypt invites her to open herself to the possibility of this "bloom-burst." She finds the invitation both frightening and attractive; the possible gain in self-realization seems matched by the likely loss of self-autonomy.

Her heightened sensuality is given point and urgency in the person of Captain Rafton, an ex-British Army officer who is stopping at the Hotel Luxor on his way to a job at Assuan. He escorts her about the sites and in all ways behaves most attentively. How he actually feels about her is not made explicit because the narration does not present his point of view, but there is no doubting his attractiveness to Helen. His presence transforms the cultural conflict she has felt between Athens and Egypt into a personal crisis. He represents the power of nature that she both fears and desires.

As a way of guarding herself against him, she admits that he is appealing but assumes that he lacks refinement. Revealing an antipathy similar to Hipparchia's, she reflects: "Almost he seemed to her, as he spoke, authentic, Roman, officer of one of the flashy and distinguished legions of the middle-aging procrastinator, Caesar" (249). For a while, her reaction to him is dominated by fear: "She suspected him of the worst. He had some power. She knew he had, suspected him, feared for it. Hoped that he hadn't, wished that he had. For how disastrous, after all, if he should turn out the most, most ordinary of ex-captains merely on his way up to Assuan on his job" (262). Yet, as they become better acquainted, she begins to think more highly of him. She notices signs of greater cultivation than she had expected. He remarks, "You're always talking about the Greeks. The Greeks came to Egypt to learn" (306). She is obliged to admit to herself the perceptiveness of this comment: "*The Greeks came to Egypt to learn.* . . . Where, if he were this common post-war officer, had he picked up these pertinent observations?" (309).

Satisfied that Captain Rafton is no boor, Helen seems to be falling in love with him. When they are together, she acts self-consciously; she accuses herself of behaving "like a gauche and awkward school-girl" (273). The height of her infatuation is reached when he takes her and another couple on a nighttime visit to some outlying tombs. The carriage ride across the desert in the moonlight, the Captain's tactful arrangement of the details, and his open expression of affection lead Helen to submit to his charm. "You will look after me, won't you?" he asks (310). She twists his ring in reply and realizes how much pleasure she takes in placing herself at his disposal, especially now that she is convinced of his refinement:

> Past, present, all the commutations of past and present (as light cast through darkened glass) were merged at one within her. The just past, the far past. She was released, as any nursemaid dallying in any garrison town (Gibraltar, Maidenhead) with any common soldier.
>
> Apparently then the Greeks *did* come to Egypt to learn. She didn't now believe he was a common soldier. She didn't care one way or the other. If Zeus takes form, wouldn't he these days, take some recognised by simple people? . . . So that she could quite happily, illiterate, superstitious, believe that he was some uncommon Power. (310-11)

However, the next morning Helen sees their relationship with a more reluctant eye. She goes sightseeing with Mary, her young friend, and clearly enjoys leading the docile girl about; she wonders if being the mate of a strong-willed man will be as pleasant. She is also surprised to learn that Mary has lost much of her enthusiasm for field trips because she too has fallen in love. She is considering marrying someone whom Helen considers merely an amusing boy. This turn of events reminds Helen of the capriciousness of sexual attraction. She takes Mary's willingness to give herself to someone ordinary as a warning that she might suffer the same fate herself. Personal freedom, even if lonesome, seems infinitely preferable to being a bond-slave in marriage. She reverts to a suspicious view of her admirer that had crossed her mind the previous evening:

> Captain Rafton's only just the most ordinary of ex-army captains on his way up to Assuan on a job. She felt exactly as one who has been under ether, that pollen dust of physical annihilators, and has come out of it. As if the whole of this strange crowded, over-taxed day had been some sort of gold and pollen, mist and lily dream, some excursion into some outre-mer where thought was transposed into form, into tall upstanding pillars, squat, heavy where the sand-coloured column ripened into a heavy swollen bud. (318)

At the end of the tale she seems determined to reject the Captain's proposal and to dismiss the whole episode as an erotic fantasy.

Conclusion

Thus does H. D. settle the amorous and cultural conflicts of her three protagonists. Although the style throughout *Palimpsest* is uniform—an impersonal narrator who at times merges with the principal character—the situations of these women are varied and plausible. The same offhand, breathless prolixity is common to them all, but the classical setting of "Hipparchia," the nervous introspection of Raymonde Ransome, and the social involvements of Helen Fairwood enable them to be distinguished easily. Each section contains monotonous stretches and is unduly long, but each is also both singular and cognate with the others. Moreover, all are marked by a high degree of empathy with the main characters and by patient skill in representing their personalities.

The dramatic conflicts in these sections are resolved in a way that indicates H. D.'s limited resourcefulness in handling psychological quandaries. Hipparchia's inability either to find a suitable lover or to follow a literary career in solitude is relieved by the sudden appearance of a wealthy girl who beseeches Hipparchia to become her traveling companion. The reader is pleased at Hipparchia's good fortune—if her patrons prove themselves to be as considerate as they seem—but he is disappointed by so adventitious and unlikely a resolution of her difficulty.

In Raymonde Ransome's section, the pertinence of H. D.'s solution is questionable. Raymonde is able to accept the treachery of her friend by viewing the situation as inevitable, as though it were a tale of Phaedra or Medea, and by freeing herself of grief through the catharsis of art. Although these responses may provide some consolation, Raymonde's situation fundamentally involves moral issues that H. D. fails to meet. Fatalism undermines morality, and art involves imperatives that face in a different direction.

"Secret Name" introduces social comedy to the palimpsest. The behavior of Helen Fairwood and her acquaintances is presented with an eye to its incongruity. Helen acts more like an adolescent than a woman in her thirties; the captain offers a copybook explanation of Egyptian culture to a scholar who pretends to be impressed; Mary and her boy friend flirt while they are touring the sites, and Mary's mother is a stereotype of the snob abroad. These effects are amusing, but they block the reader from taking the group seriously. Yet H. D. clearly wishes Helen, at least, to be given serious attention: like Hipparchia and Raymonde Ransome, she is meant to illustrate the problems of a sensitive, independent-minded woman. Like the other women, she also has a penchant for seeing cultural conflicts reflected in ordinary incidents. However, since her inclination to read large meanings into small circumstances seems more ridiculous than profound, her cultural broodings produce a more comical than philosophical effect. The reader is placed in the uncomfortable position of realizing that his reaction to the narration is probably different from the one intended by H. D.

II Hedylus

Hedylus, appearing midway in the sequence of H. D.'s fiction, resembles *Palimpsest*, anticipates *Bid Me to Live*, and also presents features entirely its own. Like the "Hipparchia" section of

Palimpsest, it is set in ancient times—the island of Samos in the third century B.C. As in all of H. D.'s fiction, a principal character is a sensitive woman trying amid uncongenial circumstances to remain faithful to transcendental ideals. Like Hipparchia, Raymonde Ransome, and, as we shall see, Julia in *Bid Me to Live*, the protagonist in *Hedylus* has been rejected in love. The unique feature of this novel (but one that brings it closer to H. D.'s personal experience) is that the rejected woman has a son. She not only suffers from loneliness but fears the responsibility of motherhood.

H. D. also breaks new ground technically in this novel: she tells the story from the point of view of both the mother and the child. H. D.'s writing is mostly about the difficulty of devoting oneself to love, beauty, and poetry. In varying degrees her protagonists share these commitments. They want to enjoy love, to live beautifully, and to write poetry. And they all find this triple crown beyond their strength.

In *Hedylus* the pursuit of these ideals is divided between a mother and her son. Although they are extraordinarily engrossed with each other—as their names Hedyle and Hedylus suggest—they are individuals; and the presentation of both their points of view increases the interest of the story. H. D.'s protagonists tend to be isolated by the unbroken flow of their subjective impressions; here the presence of two central characters grants the reader at least an interior and an external view of each of them. This technique also helps to dramatize the psychological themes of the novel. Instead of being conveyed only through the consciousness of a single character, they are objectified in the behavior of two. The reader gains a second character-in-depth and a livelier sense of each one's difficulties.

The title, *Hedylus*, is the name of a poet of the third century B.C., mentioned in "The Garland" of Meleager. H. D. cites the reference in an epigraph: "The wild field-flowers of Hedylus and/Posidippus with Sikeledes' anemones." Nothing more is known about him. Upon this allusion, H. D. builds the entire tale, just as she had done in "Hipparchia" and in her lyrics based upon fragments from Sappho. She makes Hedylus a young man living on the island of Samos. Posidippus and Sikeledes are his friends and fellow poets. He is an illegitimate child; his mother Hedyle had brought him from Athens to Samos ten years earlier, when she had become the mistress of Douris, king of the island.

Both mother and son are full of anxiety. Hedyle is worried about losing her beauty; she is scornful of her royal lover, possessive and critical of her son—at once jealous of his interests and ambitious for his fame. Hedylus is overshadowed by his mother; although he is afraid to leave her, he resents her influence over him. He wants to be a poet, but he fears that his popular work is trivial and his serious work vapid. He aspires to grandeur, but he suspects that his friends find him ridiculous.

Both Hedyle and Hedylus lack a sense of self-identity. They are confused about themselves and unsure of their social position. Hedyle's father was a Sceptic philosopher who sought to destroy traditional beliefs; and, she recalls, "We never knew our mother" (11). Hedylus reminds himself that "there was just one thing he couldn't say to Hedyle—'I've never had a father'" (15). He reflects bitterly, "I am a bastard. I am a bastard in the court of Douris. I am a bastard in the court of beauty" (38).

Hedyle considers herself a victim of the war chariots of Philip of Macedon, who had "undermined the intellectual integrity as well as the mere material fortresses of Athens" (2). She is proud of her native city and wishes to be known as "the Athenian," but she admits that its glory has passed. After her father had died of the plague, she had immersed herself in the decadent society of Athens for several years. Then, when Douris offered her and her child—even she is not sure who the father is—hospitality on Samos, she had accepted. At the Samian court "she had no authentic 'position.' . . . Some said she was an 'indifferent prostitute,' some said a 'queen in hiding,' some said a 'goddess.'" (31)

Hedylus works "helping Douris in his monumental history" (21). However, he realizes that his position depends upon his mother's. He feels her domination so strongly that he exclaims: "My name, my name, my name. What is my name anyway? I am enclosed in Hedylus the son of Hedyle. Hedyle still encloses me as if I never were born" (86). Hedyle thwarts him by considering everything done on Samos provincial, compared to the eclipsed culture of Athens. She criticizes his manners, his verse, his friends, and his eagerness to be independent.

Their relationship is mutually destructive. Trying to keep Hedylus under her influence has exhausted Hedyle and restricted her personal life. Her happiness depends entirely upon her son's success, but by driving him too hard she hampers his growth. She frustrates herself and paralyzes him. Time makes matters worse; the more she withdraws from society in order to watch over him, the more he feels that she cannot do without him and the more he resents his predicament. Yet, through timidity and a childish sense of duty, he is unwilling to free himself. Her possessiveness keeps him from the selfhood that alone can please her.

The breaking of this deadlock is the heart of the novel. Within a few hours—the entire narration extends only from evening to the following dawn—unforeseen events liberate both mother and son. Although these events are fortuitous and their impact upon Hedyle and Hedylus quite unexpected, the climax is presented as auspicious for their future.

The arrival of Demetrius, an Athenian delegate on his way to Alexandria, initiates the action. Douris offers him hospitality and plans a banquet and a poetry recitation in his honor. This plan upsets Hedyle, because Demetrius has been one of her lovers—she assures Hedylus that Demetrius is not his father. His name "brought her superficial casual memory; corridors crowded with banqueters, occasional unexpected shower of rose leaves, and an uplifted naked arm that waved from a stone basin. Demetrius had used his pretended love of beauty to ornament his orgies" (5). Hedylus, noticing his mother's nervousness, decides not to attend the gathering. Because he has distressed her lately by making friends with Irene, a young girl spending a season on the island, and by talking of going to Alexandria, he does not wish to trouble her any further.

Instead, he makes his way to a ledge on a cliff overlooking the sea. There he has hidden his finest poems. He reads two of them aloud, burns a few that dissatisfy him, feels momentarily like throwing himself into the sea, and then is startled from his self-absorption by the appearance of a man in a boat. A stranger has overheard him reciting his poems.

After they greet each other, Hedylus makes courteous inquiries in order to conceal his embarrassment at being found declaiming his own verse and also to satisfy his curiosity about the stranger. The man says little, but from the outset Hedylus is fascinated by him. He seems self-possessed and imperious, obviously a cultivated person. In fact, his bearing and his sudden appearance combine with Hedylus' yearning for a father and with his preoccupation with myths of transformation to make the boy believe that the stranger is a god:

> The man, Hedylus mused, not daring yet to lift his eyes and face the stranger, was (he knew infallibly) fully evolved, the man and the god, each alive, each alert to each contingency. The man was alive, but sheltering the god; the god was sheltering the man. They fitted each other, sword and perfect scabbard. (88-89)

The stranger invites Hedylus to have supper with him, and their talk—a monologue by Hedylus punctuated by the older man's laconic observations—sustains Hedylus' faith that he is in the company of a god. Even the fact that the stranger is a merchant-explorer on his way to India does not dissuade Hedylus, because he remembers that the gods always appear in some mundane disguise, frequently the most unlikely, in order to conceal their identity from the vulgar. Their effulgence is recognized only by men with some affinity for the divine. Actually, nothing that the stranger says hints of divinity; it is his benign self-composure that suggests a deity to the fatherless poet. Hedylus trusts him completely and confides his deepest anxieties to him. As they sit together, he senses "an unassailable beauty as of gullwings" (113). Later, he tells Irene about his experience; and when she asks, "Who was it that you saw, then?" he replies, "Helios" (150).

From the outset, the stranger is sympathetic to Hedylus. He comments favorably upon his poetry: "'Your writing has only half expressed you. . . . One sees the struggle of some innate force. It breaks out at brief intervals'" (98). "'Your imagery was excellent,'" he adds in a "courteous, low-toned, continued dissertation on the poetry" (102). This praise draws tears of gratitude and humility from Hedylus. The "god" also advises him about his mother and Irene. He helps him to understand the nature of the two women, and he encourages him to act independently for their sake as well as his own. He even invites Hedylus to accompany him to India as his secretary.

This encounter frees Hedylus from self-doubt. The stranger's advice has the force of a divine revelation. Hedylus feels that he has been blessed by a god. He is no longer an illegitimate boy but an honored man. He feels reborn: "he seemed now to have been made, by the mere physical or spiritual emanation of the man beside him, one entire and concrete entity" (109). The effects of his regeneration are immediate. Upon leaving the stranger's apartment, he "emerged with exquisite pain from the dead grey cocoon of the old Hedylus" (135). He acts resolutely with his fellow poets Posidippus and Sikeledes. When they tell him that Demetrius wishes to establish the three of them as poets in Alexandria and that their boat will leave at dawn, Hedylus agrees to go.

His new relationship with his mother is more startling. Arriving home to tell her that he is bound for Alexandria, he discovers that he is no longer in awe of her. "This devastating fracture with his mother" (148) causes him almost to be condescending toward her: "He could, in his soul, say now, sing now, 'You are my enemy, my mother; you are my enemy, my mother.' He would, must, for that very flame of passionate discovery, therefore spare this wraith of grey impotence. He must spare, in order fully to escape from her" (137). Realizing that "they moved now absolutely and finally in separate orbits" (140), he leaves to join his friends aboard Demetrius' ship.

After Hedylus has gone, Hedyle accepts his emancipation with surprising equanimity. Though she is grieved by his curtness, she reminds herself that his liberation has been her ultimate goal. Treating him severely was the unavoidable consequence of being obliged to prepare him for the world: " 'I could have kept the child by wounding him, blunting his fervid intellect. I saw from the first he had it. . . . You can't love a boy and bring it up a sword . . . a solid weapon . . . when he hasn't got a father. . . . I had to put a sword in his hand so that he could fight, so that when necessary he could fight me' " (154). Now that Hedylus has asserted his independence, she realizes what a relief it is to be free of parental responsibility: "Her own son had been her standard, her threat, her constant heart-ache. She was glad, with some curious sloughing-off of spirit, now he had gone. . . . Her head felt as if some heavy helmet had been lifted from it" (158).

She is then visited by the stranger, whose solicitude for Hedylus, it seems, has not been entirely fortuitous. Hedyle greets him as Demion of Olympia, her intimate friend from the time Hedylus was one year old. When she was pregnant with Hedylus, her first impulse was to have an abortion: the circumstances of her life made childbearing seem impossible. However, while resting one day on a rock outside Sunium, she placed the affair in the hands of the gods. If a sign were given, she would have the child. A grass-snake appeared, and she took its presence to mean that the child was to be favored by Helios. Hedylus was born, and a year later she met Demion. Like Hedylus many years afterward, she immediately felt a divine quality about him:

> "You were the first man, just human-shouldered mortal, who had asked tenderly of my child. O, I was very silly. I was so weak, so stricken by the plague, Demion, that I made you an immortal. . . . You saw me as a lover. I was so ill, so childish, so surprised that I made a god of you." (172)

Although Hedyle seems aware that Demion is a god of her own making, she acknowledges the help that he has been to her. "In a world of constant wreckage, flowers being broken, frost smiting knife-wise, evil marring beauty" (160), he has symbolized the godlike qualities of mankind. During the more than ten years since their last meeting, the mere knowledge of his existence has supported her. She tells him: " 'My belief in your identity with beauty has held me earth-bound. My body but for that would have soon dissolved, rotted into the baser elements' " (182). During an era marked by a growing indifference, even hostility, to the divine—"Gods now were treated like vermin in low-lying marshes, to be dried out by sterile philosophic speculation or to be drained away like fetid useless water" (82)—she has seen a deity in Demion. This experience has enabled her to overcome scandal and loneliness.

Now, as though to demonstrate his power anew, Demion has liberated both mother and son. She assures him that she will continue to feel his presence in every beautiful aspect of life. " 'My love for you is linked with an absolute illiterate faith in the materialization, in the reality, of beauty' " (184). He returns her compliment—and ends the novel—by bestowing upon her son the epithet of which she has been most proud, "the Athenian."

As a novel, *Hedylus* is both compelling and weak. Its attractiveness consists largely of features already mentioned: the presentation of the consciousness of both a mother and a son, each struggling for individuality and handicapped by difficult circumstances. The conflict between parent and child is a subject as perennial in literature as in life, and the depiction of it in an ancient setting adds to its interest. H. D., who rarely referred in her work to her experience as a mother, dramatizes the problems of rearing a child in the absence of the father. Her actual daughter was transformed into a fictional son probably because of the greater evocativeness of the mother-son pattern and also because a mother's conflict between showing affection and preparing a child for independence seems more urgent in the case of a son.

The inherent appeal of this subject is increased by making the son a poet. The novel thereby becomes "a portrait of the artist as a young man," as well as the story of tensions between parent and child. Here, too, H. D. was able to draw upon her personal experience. She wisely used her understanding of these two situations to expand her literary range. Always an autobiographical writer, she was able in *Hedylus* to present the consciousness of two central characters.

Unfortunately, these potential advantages are outweighed by several weaknesses. Hedylus, intended to be the most important character, fades beside Hedyle. His anxieties, aspirations, and finally his emancipation leave no vivid impression. He remains a pale, vague figure whose departure seems as unreal as his presence.

This weakness would be of minor consequence if Hedyle were stronger, but the more she is seen and heard, the less impressive she becomes. Her inadequacy is unlike Hedylus': he lacks substance; she has a great deal but of the wrong sort. She is presented as a sophisticated, elegant beauty, a "queen in hiding." She seems rather like a village actress trying to play the part. Although the opening lines of the novel aim at establishing her superiority, they achieve an effect closer to caricature:

> Hedyle of Athens let go the polished mirror. She said, "Eyes, nose, mouth. I've seen them all so often. Everybody has an eye,—eyes, I mean,—nose, mouth. I am just like all the others." She ran her incredibly slender index along the back of the mirror, and her fingers told her of curved line of exquisite symmetry, of tenuous, curled vine-tendril and somewhere (she felt for it) the slightly too heavy incised, frankly rampant grape-bunch. "This mirror is like me, inconsistent in particulars. I've been here too long to believe in beauty. Beauty went when the Macedonians undermined our earthworks. Sometimes it's almost too pitiful to watch them at it, all these semi-Asiatic barbarians trying to play at beauty. If Douris weren't so frankly entertaining, I would leave him." (1)

Her reaction to Hedylus' departure lurches from sentimentality to bookishness: "'I'm not crying. I did everything I could do. . . . To tell the child I loved him would have reduced my staid determination to another formula. It would have been not Athene with young Ion or Erechtheus, bringing him to power and strength in order to serve Athens'" (154).

The conversations between Hedyle and Hedylus are also disappointing. They seem tedious and self-conscious; yet the narrator finds them exhilarating: "Their conversation now as always was flippant dialogue, snap and spark and exact pause preceding answer. They seemed to count their pauses like trained actors" (13-14). The only relief from this combination of the characters' dullness and the narrator's adulation is that occasionally the mother and son speak of each other more accurately: he finds her tiresome, and she finds him callow.

In addition to the weakness of the main characters, there are other drawbacks. The reader's credulity is overtaxed not only by the arrival of Demion just in time to resolve a family crisis but by the godlike impression he makes on Hedylus—exactly parallel to the impression he made on Hedyle years before. This ending reminds the reader of the unconvincing resolution to Hipparchia's troubles. Moreover, the minor characters, the setting, and several details of the plot are insubstantial. Seen through the consciousness of the mother and her son, the world appears vague; and practically no other direct impression is given. The reader is limited to the two main characters, and they are inadequate. The conclusion is inescapable that for want of livelier storytelling, sharper characterization, and more controlled diction, H. D. fumbled an attractive possibility.

III Bid Me to Live

Although *Bid Me to Live* was not published until 1960, thirty-two years after *Hedylus*, it closely resembles the two earlier novels in subject and manner. The protagonist, Julia Ashton, is a distraught woman, like Hipparchia, Raymonde Ransome, and Hedyle. Living in London during World War I, she faces daily the threat of air raids and the collapse of her marriage. The novel describes the disintegration of her personal life and her struggle to build a new one. As in H. D.'s other novels, an impersonal narrator presents the story from the protagonist's point of view. At times, the separation between the narrator and Julia disappears entirely.

Nevertheless, *Bid Me to Live* strikes the reader with greater impact than *Palimpsest* and *Hedylus*. H. D. makes more effective use of descriptive details and direct quotations in establishing the setting and the supporting characters. As a result, it is easier to respond sympathetically to Julia. Receiving some objective corroboration of her view of events, the reader is less apt to be confused or unsure of her reliability.

Also, this novel has greater power because H. D. deals openly with an experience that functions clandestinely in the others: a woman's being rejected in love. All of her heroines have known this experience, but only in *Bid Me to Live* is it placed at the center of the work and presented as a crushing humiliation. In *Palimpsest*, although Marius finds Hipparchia cold and finally leaves her, H. D. emphasizes Hipparchia's contempt for his lust. Their relationship becomes a symbol of a clash between cultures: Hipparchia, a Greek, sees Marius as a typical Roman. In "Murex," Raymonde Ransome has lost her husband to another woman, but ten years before the action of the story. Helen Fairwood in "Secret Name" is not explicitly involved with this theme, but she has been married and her reluctance to accept Captain Rafton's attentions results from her fear of being again victimized by love. Similarly in *Hedylus*, although Hedyle is not concerned about love personally, all her anxieties spring from her obligation to rear an illegitimate child.

The behavior of these women can be understood only by taking their unhappy love affairs into account. However, the reader finds them, except for Julia in *Bid Me to Live*, engaged with other matters and, at the most, either glancing at their love affairs from a safe distance or rationalizing their humiliation. The result is a disharmony between their behavior and their situation. Their deepest motives are inadequately admitted to the reader and to themselves.

Only in *Bid Me to Live* are theme and action harmonized. Like H. D.'s other women, Julia Ashton is a rejected lover, but, unlike them, she is seen being rejected. Probably hers was the story that H. D. was impelled to write from the outset but for a long time found too painful to handle. In *Palimpsest* and in *Hedylus*, this love-trauma exists in the background and weakens the story because its presence is not openly acknowledged. It is presented in *Bid Me to Live* without evasiveness.

H. D. appears to be using the painful experience of her married life for the first time. The episodes about World War I in Aldington's autobiography, *Life for Life's Sake*,[4] in Cournos'

Autobiography,[5] and in Nehls' biography of Lawrence[6] prepare the reader to identify every important character in H. D.'s novel. For example, it seems certain that Julia Ashton and her husband Rafe represent H. D. and Aldington, and that Frederick and Elsa represent Lawrence and his wife Frieda. These fictional representations seem remarkably close to fact, but gauging their accuracy may be left to biographers. What matters in this discussion is the literary quality of the novel and the contribution made to it by the use of an autobiographical source. In this respect, *Bid Me to Live* is impressive and clearly superior to H. D.'s earlier fiction. Julia Ashton, the character from whose point of view the story is told, possesses a convincing personality. Her individuality is sufficiently well established to account for her behavior, unusual though it is at times.

Julia is an idealistic young woman whose happiness has been lost through a series of disappointments. She is an American living in England, married to Rafe Ashton, an Englishman. Both poets, they had planned to make their lives an ode to beauty. They were to write, to travel, and to give no hostages to middle-class custom. For a time, their hopes were realized. They visited the Continent; they translated the classics and read modern literature. They felt like the devoted lovers of Herrick's madrigal "To Anthea" (the source of H. D.'s title):

> Bid me to live, and I will live
>   Thy Protestant to be:
> Or bid me love, and I will give
>   A loving heart to thee.
>
> . . . .
>
> Thou art my life, my love, my heart,
>   The very eyes of me:
> And hast command of every part,
>   To live and die for thee.

Then nature and society ended their idyl: Julia became pregnant, and World War I started—"superficially entrenched, they were routed out by the sound of air-craft" (11). She had already suffered a miscarriage—an ordeal that left "a gap in her consciousness, a sort of black hollow, a cave, a pit of blackness" (12). In addition, she had been warned not to have a child, at least until after the war. Subsequently, she found sexual intercourse painful and frightening. Meanwhile, Rafe had become an army officer. During his training period, she had followed him from camp to camp. Then he had been sent to the Western Front, and she had settled in a flat in London.

When the novel opens, Julia has been living in their flat for some time. Rafe is on furlough from France, but he and Julia have been unable to revive their old relationship, and Julia has come to accept its loss as permanent. "She had married him when he was another person. That was the catch, really" (16). Before, he was her poet-lover; now he is a "hearty, oversexed . . . young officer on leave" (46). The difference is so great that "he would be almost nearer, once he had gone, than he was now" (24). She can write letters to the husband she remembers—letters that he treasures—but she is inadequate to the man he has become. She ruefully admits that, in their new relationship, " 'bid me to live and I will live' was just a song put to music out of the Elizabethan book of madrigals, somewhere over there on that shelf" (129).

Their estrangement is complicated by two new relationships: each has turned to someone else for the comfort that they cannot find in each other. Rafe has taken a mistress, Bella; Julia enters an intimate correspondence with Frederick, a friend of the Ashtons. Rafe insists that Bella, who lives upstairs, is merely a partner in sex: " 'Listen,' he said, 'it's perfectly clear, I love you, I desire *l'autre*' " (56). While home on leave, he wants to forget what the war has done to his life; Bella provides a sensual narcotic, whereas Julia only increases his awareness of lost hopes. Yet, rather like Marius in "Hipparchia," after he has been with Bella, he seeks Julia; and when he is in battle, he thinks of her.

Frederick, called Frederico or simply Rico, is a writer with a notorious reputation for "those heady sex-expositions that nobody would publish" (76). He is married to Elsa, an aristocratic German woman who has abandoned her children and her first husband. Rico and Elsa have no money and have been living in various places on the kindness of friends. Recently they have been on the coast of Cornwall, but the police, suspecting that they were planning to signal German ships, forced them to leave. Julia has come to their rescue by inviting them to share her flat.

Julia has found in her correspondence with Rico a substitute for her lost relationship with Rafe. His nature seems in tune with her own—they both aim at transforming their passionate response to life into art, and they both jealously guard the autonomy of their creative spirit. In addition, he has praised her poems. Their letters have enabled her "to tune-in to another dimension, a world where she walked alone with an image and that image was Rico. Truly, yes, she loved him but loved him in another dimension, out of the body" (68-69). Moreover, he has recognized the painfulness of her life with Rafe, urging her to "kick over your tiresome house of life" (61). He has even promised, "We will go away together where the angels come down to earth" (57). Although what he means by this promise remains unclear to Julia, her self-confidence is revived by his interest in her: "The fact that Rico wanted her, no matter how idealistically she might translate his letters, meant that there was something there, something that was wanted. . . . it was now as if this cerebral contact had renewed her" (58).

To her surprise, Julia recognizes that these extra-marital relationships have brought herself and Rafe closer together. The mutual accommodation of their needs has lessened the tension between them. Bella's physical comfort for Rafe and Rico's spiritual support for Julia allow them to stop making impossible demands of each other and to enjoy what remains of their marriage. She takes satisfaction in their continuing desire to be candid toward each other. After Rafe has been with Bella, he and Julia chat amiably of their earlier times together. Julia calls "the straightforward way they had of telling each other everything" the "Christ-child of their battered integrity," and she wistfully reminds herself that "in heaven, there is neither marriage nor giving in marriage" (62).

This convenient arrangement is short-lived; it crumbles under pressure from both sides. Bella makes greater demands upon Rafe; she complains to Julia, " 'He can't have it both ways' " and " 'You tyrannize his spirit' " (47). At about the same time, the arrival of Rico and his wife puts Julia's more ethereal love affair to the test. Almost immediately, Rico leads Julia to believe that he wishes to become her lover:

> There were the usual tea-cups. Rico didn't smoke. Elsa chain-smoked till all the cigarettes had given out. Rico said, "You are there for all eternity, our love is written in blood," he said, "for all eternity." But whose love? His and Elsa's? No—that was taken for granted. It was to be a perfect triangle, Elsa acquiesced.
>
> "This will leave me free," she muttered in her German guttural. (78)

Despite Julia's anxiety about sexual intercourse, she seems ready to accept; she awaits only a sign that Rico wants her to come to his room. He has an opportunity the next day, when they are alone in her flat:

> She got up; as if at a certain signal, she moved toward him; she edged the small chair toward his chair. She sat at his elbow, a child waiting for instruction. Now was the moment to answer his amazing proposal of last night, his "for all eternity," She put out her hand. Her hand touched his sleeve. He shivered, he seemed to move back, move away, like a hurt animal, there was something untamed, even the slight touch of her hand on his sleeve seemed to have annoyed him. (81)

His physical withdrawal stuns Julia and unmistakably defines the limits of their relationship. She decides that they cannot be lovers because they are both unwilling to risk their self-autonomy. Intimacy between them is possible at a safe distance—a "cerebral contact." Apparently, Rico enjoys a relationship with Elsa that he will neither place in jeopardy nor attempt to achieve with anyone else. This observation is confirmed for Julia a few evenings later when he assigns parts in a game of charades: Rafe and Bella are Adam and Eve, Julia is the Tree of Life, Elsa is the Serpent, and Rico is God! Shortly after, Rico and Elsa move to other temporary quarters.

Following Rico's departure, Rafe's affair with Bella enters a new phase. Bella refuses to play the role of concubine any longer and demands that Rafe choose between herself and Julia. Rafe tries to temporize, at least until the war is over, but Bella insists and shortly succeeds in vanquishing Julia completely.

Julia's defeat involves an ironic twist of justice. She has condoned Rafe's adultery as long as she has not been forced to give him up entirely and as long as the affair is carried on discreetly in Bella's room. However, Julia has become fearful that the genteel landladies, going from room to room to announce air raids, will come upon Rafe in Bella's bed. To avoid this embarrassment and possibly their all being evicted from the house, Julia tells the lovers to stay in her flat when a raid seems likely. They take her at her word, and when she returns from the theater the following evening, she discovers them *in flagrante.* She manages to apologize for disturbing them, but inwardly she is crushed. The ignominy of her position suddenly numbs her:

"the end came, when she no longer felt anything. That was a strange moment, almost a new cosmos had rayed out from her, feeling nothing as she stood in the door, as she stepped forward into a room. . . . Drag husband, mistress out of your own bed. . . . She had felt nothing at all" (116-17).

A short time later, Bella's victory is made total when Rafe decides to return to her after the war. Ironically again, he explains to Julia that he feels bound to Bella because she wants a child. He adds that although he is choosing Bella, he owes his life to Julia's loyalty during the war and even that he finds her the most beautiful woman he has ever known. But he leaves her.

Julia feels that she has lost everything—child, husband, and Rico. She feels empty, drained of life, "very cold, very old" (127). "She already had died. Already she was out of her body" (119). Recent events seem like a crucible in which she has been totally neutralized: "The chemicals in the test-tube had done their job. They had projected her out, the same, different, the same, a little clearer, a little harder, a little (to quote Rico) more dangerously frozen" (128). "She had been crystallized out and the human throb and beat that had been her head, her heart, was quiet" (131).

Julia is resurrected from this death-in-life by Vane, a young composer who, in Rico's charade, had been assigned the role of the Angel at the Gate. For a while Elsa had seemed interested in him, but nothing had come of their relationship. Rico had never worried about his wife's vagary; he understood that she, the Serpent, wished to be related only to himself, God. However, he had seen an affinity between Julia and Vane—the Tree of Life and the Angel. More realistically, Vane is a Scotsman with a weak heart. Exempt from military duty, he keeps to his music, living in London and in Cornwall, where he has recently been host to Rico and Elsa. He says, "I want two things, I want to finish my opera and I want a beautiful relationship with a woman" (115). By "beautiful" he means platonic. With fine instinct, he takes Julia to dinner and invites her to go with him to Cornwall.

She gratefully accepts his invitation. At a moment when she feels annihilated, he offers her life on terms she is willing to meet. He makes no sexual demands, regarding her only as a sensitive fellow artist; she believes that in Cornwall she will recover from the oppressiveness of London. She later tells Rafe of the plan, explaining that she and Vane do not love each other but are "just two people who seem to belong together" (132). Compared with Rafe and Bella, she sees herself and Vane at "the other end of the sliding-scale or the other end of the thermometer or the other side of the map or the other side of the world" (132).

As Julia has hoped, her stay in Cornwall is restorative. Vane's cottage is on the coast, and she enjoys walking over paths broken centuries ago by Celtic tin miners. The salty air nurtures plants she has never seen before; she takes pleasure in their shape and fragrance. The earth seems fresh, the rocks strong and enduring, and the mist like a cold balm. She rejoices that she has "walked out of a dream, the fog and fever, the constant threat from the air, the constant reminder of death and suffering . . . into reality" (146). For her, reality means nature viewed pantheistically. She finds that the severity of the elements—wind, rock, and sea—braces her spirit. Unlike society, nature is an "inhuman element, a divine element. It did not play vile tricks, it did not shatter windows, it did not break nerves. Rather, it sustained the being of man" (159).

In this mood and living amid the remains of ancient times, she takes a long view of life. The landscape seems charged with clues to the enigma of existence—"symbolic like a temple wall-painting" (147). She senses its meaning: "Somewhere, somehow, a pattern repeated itself, life advances in a spiral. . . . All this was meant to happen. It was pre-ordained" (148). She sees human affairs as benevolently determined: all behavior is inevitable and at the same time it manifests a divine spirit in whose inscrutable mastery the individual may trust. She now believes that "everything that had happened in London had been bound to happen. It had been necessary. Those who had precipitated its happening were each separately blessed by her" (145-46). She is pleased to realize that Rafe and Bella and Rico have been the agents of her spiritual awakening!

For the future—she and Vane understand that their life together is temporary—Julia intends to devote herself to writing. Her faith in beauty has been renewed; as an artist, she will celebrate the loveliness and transcendental intimations of nature. She trusts that her sensitive, brooding passiveness that has been a burden in her personal relations will be good for her creative life. At the moment she is translating a Greek chorus sequence, laboring "to get what she wanted, to hew and chisel those lines, to maintain or suggest some cold artistry" (162). She is also preparing a new volume of lyrics that she assumes will please her small group of readers. However, what she really seeks is "to explain how it is that the rose is neither red nor white, but a pale *gloire*" (176). By *gloire* she appears to mean the ideal spirit that exists in nature and that artists attempt to reveal in their work.

She expresses these hopes in a lengthy journal entry that comprises the closing portion of the novel. It is in the form of a letter to Rico, even though she plans neither to send it to him nor ever to see him again. It is for herself alone, and so she writes candidly of the part he is continuing to play in her life. For her, he has become an abstract force—the divine element in art and nature. In this guise, he truly bids her to live. By recognizing and valuing what he represents, she unites herself to him eternally. In human terms, she decides that their relationship failed because each was searching for a mother-figure rather than a mate; their needs were so similar that they could not help each other. She likens his creative impulse to Van Gogh's: both are tormented in their struggle to give expression to love. She feels that ultimately he will succeed. Recently he had told her that he had seen her "'singing in a dream. I woke and found my face wet with tears'" (184). This confession proves to Julia that he cares for her and is responsive to love. She cannot doubt that this openness to love will enrich his art.

On this plane of affectionate idealism, H. D. concludes the novel. Altogether it is a poignant work: Julia's marital difficulties compel sympathy, and her effort to reorganize her life has the reader's strongest support. However, the narrative is unconvincing in several respects. Julia's relationship with Rico is perplexing; her attitude toward him is clear, but his view of her is uncertain. The character of Vane is also difficult to accept. Even though he is meant to be a pallid foil to Rafe's sensual and Rico's cerebral passion, he falls short of embodying even this frail type of person; he is, therefore, more a solution to a problem than a man. Like the young girl at the end of "Hipparchia," he exists solely to relieve Julia's dilemma, but the person given this important role needs to be rendered more plausibly. Rico names him the Angel at the Gate; unintentionally, he suggests Vane's function in the novel: a *deus ex machina*, a heroine-saving device.

Moreover, the resolution reached by Julia is troublesome. Her recovery from despair gladdens the reader, but her acceptance of a doctrine of benevolent fatalism is disappointing because it is too easy and insubstantial a way to settle complex issues. It renders pointless all concern for personal and social ethics; yet the attractiveness of the early part of the novel is that it arouses such concern. By becoming an optimistic fatalist, Julia demonstrates more spirit than intelligence.

This defect symbolizes a characteristic of *Bid Me to Live* that the reader cannot fully assess. Julia seems full of self-delusion and fear. The problem for the reader is to decide whether or not H. D. intended to dramatize these traits. Some passages suggest that she did, but more often the exhibition of Julia's weakness seems unintended. As a result, the reader suspects that—as in the case of Hipparchia, Hedyle, Raymonde, and Helen Fairwood—he thinks less of Julia than H. D. does. This novel, like the others, is weakened by the fact that H. D. seems imperfectly aware of the limitations of her principal characters.

CHAPTER 4

Red Roses for Bronze

IN 1931, *Red Roses for Bronze*[1] was published, containing twenty original poems and three verse translations. Appearing six years after *Collected Poems*, this volume generally resembles the earlier. However, it contains several poems that show a distinct change in style. H. D.'s previous work consisted typically of concisely rendered images drawn from nature and the classics. Her new manner is more explicit, colloquial, and diffuse. She uses everyday, commonplace diction, even though the setting remains a highly stylized version of the ancient world. Her intention seems to be to make poetry of the monologue of a self-preoccupied, high-strung woman.

The themes of *Red Roses for Bronze* are the same as those in *Collected Poems*. Love, art, and beauty are still the central topics, and the difficulty of achieving these goals is still the main concern. As in *Collected Poems*, love is desired and feared; it is viewed as offering the finest but the most painful human experience. Love is also recognized as a strong spur to art; yet the personal involvements of love are seen as distractions to the artist. Moreover, H. D. finds the vulgarity of the modern scene repellent to both the lover and the artist. She feels that only nature can be relied upon to gratify the esthetic sense—not the emasculated nature of gardens but the grandeur of high peaks and rockbound shores. However, like love, nature isolates its admirers from society and discourages them from art. Thus in *Red Roses for Bronze*, H. D. shifts from one dilemma to another, just as she did in *Collected Poems*. No reconciliation of these problems is achieved, but the terms imposed by each are vividly established.

The presence of virtually the same themes in all the poems considered thus far gives the reader an excellent opportunity to evaluate the stylistic innovation H. D. made in *Red Roses for Bronze*. Regrettably, the new style is less successful than the old; the best poems of the new volume are in the manner of *Col-*

lected Poems. There is, for example, in "If You Will Let Me Sing" the fusion of succinctness and classicism characteristic of her early work:

If you will let me sing,
that God will be
gracious to each of us,
who found his own wild Daphne
in a tree,
who set
on desolate plinth,
image
of Hyacinth.

The same traits are successfully fused in "Triplex" in which the poet prays that she may combine the virtues of Athena, Aphrodite, and Artemis. The poem ends:

Let them grow side by side in me,
these three;
violets,
dipped purple in stark Attic light,
rose,
scorched (on Cyprus coast)
ambrosial white
and wild
exquisite hill-crocus
from Arcadian snows.

In "All Mountains," she expresses her preference for an arduous rather than a comfortable life. Using images drawn from nature, she resigns to others the "earth/crushed flat/with crude layers/of fitted square"; for herself she wants "the islands of the upper air,/all mountains/and the towering mountain trees." In "Epitaph" she presents a three-sided view of herself:

So I may say,
"I died of living,
having lived one hour";

so they may say,
"she died soliciting
illicit fervour";

so you may say,
"Greek flower; Greek ecstasy
reclaims for ever

one who died
following
intricate songs' lost measure."

These poems illustrate H. D.'s work at its best: spare, intense, and evocative. In them she demonstrates her talent for objectifying her themes of the inner life in meaningful images.

H. D.'s unexpected diffusiveness in *Red Roses for Bronze* is most apparent in the title poem, as well as "In the Rain," "Chance Meeting," "Wine Bowl," "Myrtle Bough," "Halcyon," and "Chance." Prolixity replaces the concentration of her earlier work. By using many short lines, divided into single words or phrases with frequent repetition, she suggests a self-centered woman talking to herself. At times the speaker seems to be using commonplace expressions deliberately in the hope of underplaying her sophistication. In "Red Roses for Bronze," for example, the protagonist wishes to sculpt the head of a handsome, godlike man. She hopes to present the bust to him as a gift that will outshine the attentions of his other admirers. In the second section, she refers to a meeting they have had:

All very well
while all the others smirked,
to turn and smile:
you thought that I might see your joke,
would do
(fault of a better)
for the moment anyhow;
you knew
that I would prove too strange, too proud,
for just the ordinary sort of come and go,
the little half-said thing,
the half-caught smile,
the subtle little sort of differentiating
between the thing that's said
and that's said not;
the "have I seen you somewhere else?
forgot? impossible,"
the half-caught back half-smile,
the interrupted nod,
"a clod
may hold the rarest flower,
so I?"

the question that's an answer
and the thing
that means that what's said
isn't answering;
this,
this,
or this,
or this thing
or this other;

This passage fails because what is intended as an ironic but moving statement is merely tiresome.

The principal weakness of these poems is triteness. Wherever this fault is avoided by the use of imagery—"In the Rain," for example—the quality rises. The protagonist, who says she is pleased that a love affair is over, tells herself that she will be free of much suffering, free to enjoy nature and society. She even prays to be ignored by Love in the future. Then she is constrained to admit that Love had made her feel alive; without it, she feels dead once more. In the fourth section, her temporary illusion that life would be joyous without love is attractively expressed:

the air
will be full of multiple wings;
the fountain-basin, bare
of ripple and circlet, will spring
into life,
will duplicate ring
on translucent ring
of amethyst water,
purple
and rare
crimson;

In the sixth section, the poem droops with colloquial commonplaces lacking in taste and imagination. The speaker is urging Love to ignore her:

Don't come there,
don't come,
you have all the world,
go anywhere,
everywhere,
you have cloak and wings and a rod,

all the paths are yours,
all, all the altars
save one,
this one
of my intimate God;
don't come near,
go here,
there,
where you will,

"Chance" illustrates further that, although the poems in this volume tend to be longer than the best of the earlier ones, they are weakened not by length but by dullness. A short poem rendered distasteful by sentimentality, it begins: "Chance says,/come here,/chance says,/can you bear/to part?/chance says,/sweetheart,/we haven't loved/for almost a year." This vulgar strain is kept up to the end: "chance says,/dear,/I'm here,/don't you want me/any more?" Conversely, "Myrtle Bough" is a long poem sustained by vivid images. Its theme and emotion are not inherently more conducive to poetry than those of "Chance," but they are realized in clear-cut details:

Then let me be a brother
to your need,
shoulder to steel-clad shoulder;
let me take
the helmet
and the buckler
and the greaves, Aristogiton,
to your slender grace;
let women fall beside us,
and men frown,
let us be soul and brother,
having won
the bitter wisdom
of Love's bitterest greed.

It is puzzling to find H. D.'s verse banal because the most obvious virtue of her work from the outset was its striking imagery. In *Red Roses for Bronze* she seems to be losing her greatest and most natural gift. To explain this loss, two reasons may be ventured. She may have begun to confuse her personal moods with creative impulses—a confusion to which introspective, autobiographical writers are especially liable. In this state, the poet assumes that a poem can be made of any strongly felt experience. He is beguiled into believing that, because he is a poet, whatever he says is poetry.

Another reason for H. D.'s use of unimaginative monologues may have been her interest in stream-of-consciousness fiction. In the novels *Palimpsest* and *Hedylus*, published between *Collected Poems* and *Red Roses for Bronze*, she tried to express the interplay of sensation, thought, and memory. The results, although interesting as technical experiments in the type of fiction being developed at the same time by Proust, Joyce, Dorothy Richardson, and Virginia Woolf, fell short of her intentions. Her themes are inadequately dramatized. In addition, long stretches of the novels are dull—for the same reason that some of the poems in *Red Roses for Bronze* are dull: the protagonists' reflections are tedious and boring. This weakness is particularly noticeable in the poems because H. D. gives no sign that she is deliberately presenting the monologues of monotonous women. Consequently, the reader charges his annoyance to H. D.'s discredit. The fault appears to be literary: H. D. had some talent for the interior monologue that is the essence of stream-of-consciousness writing, but her major strength was in image-making. When she shifted from a controlled use of metaphor to an introspective use of the vernacular, the results were commonplace. Thus, at its best her verse is luminous; for example, in an early poem, "Leda":

Through the deep purple
of the dying heat
of sun and mist,
the level ray of sun-beam
has caressed
the lily with dark breast,
and flecked with richer gold
its golden crest.

In "Chance" it drops to the triteness of "sweetheart,/we haven't loved/for almost a year,/can you bear/this loneliness?" Clearly, her verse is weakest when she tries to express realistically the consciousness of the inner life. This fact suggests that her interest in stream-of-consciousness fiction was unfortunate for her poetry. It won her a minor place in the development of the modern novel, but it led her to deviate from her natural poetic sensibility.

CHAPTER 5

Translations and Adaptations

I *Translations*

ENTIRELY in accord with H. D.'s cultural outlook is her deep interest in translating the classics. Her lifelong admiration for ancient times and her knowledge of Greek and Latin would almost inevitably have involved some translating, whether she chose to publish the results or not. Moreover, in her novels, two important characters are working on translations, and their remarks present a virtual statement of principles for this enterprise.

In the "Hipparchia" section of *Palimpsest*, Hipparchia is translating from Greek to Latin. She realizes that it is impossible to render a work justly in another language if the cultures that they express are incompatible. In her case, she finds it a desecration to attempt translating a song by Moero. Her contempt for the Romans is epitomized in her conviction that Latin cannot convey the delicacy of the Greek lyric:

> The translation in the heavier language read faulty, repetitive. It was as if a light that had been burning in clear agate was now set in granite. . . . As soon think of putting the run and vowelled throat of a mountain stream into chiseled stone, as to translate the impassive, passionate yet so coldly restrained Greek utterance into this foreign language. . . . She would quote it entire in Greek. The Greek words, inset in her manuscript, would work terrific damage. She almost saw the Dictator's palace overpowered by it. (99-100)

Julia Ashton, in *Bid Me to Live*, does not doubt the potentiality of English as a vehicle for Greek, but she is having trouble making a translation that does not violate either language:

> She brooded over each word, as if to hatch it. Then she tried to forget each word, for "translations" enough existed and she was no scholar. She did not want to "know" Greek in that sense.

She was like one blind who knows an inner light, a reality that the outer eye cannot grasp. She was arrogant and she was intrinsically humble before this discovery. Her own.

Anyone can translate the meaning of the word. She wanted the shape, the feel of it, the character of it, as if it had been freshly minted. She felt that the old manner of approach was as toward hoarded treasure, but treasure that had passed through too many hands, had been too carefully assessed by the grammarians. She wanted to coin new words. (162-63)

H. D.'s ambitions were undoubtedly encouraged by her friend and literary mentor, Ezra Pound. At the outset of his career, his omnivorous reading habits and his talent for foreign languages prompted him to make translations and to evaluate the ones currently being done. With his usual brusque didacticism, he was soon proclaiming that "Greek in English remains almost wholly unsuccessful."[1] He explained: "It seems to me that English translators have gone wide in two ways, first in trying to keep every adjective, when obviously many adjectives in the original have only melodic value, secondly they have been deaved with syntax; have wasted time, involved their English, trying first to evolve a definite logical structure for the Greek and secondly to preserve it, *and all its grammatical relations*, in English."[2]

To correct this tendency, he presented some of his own work —translations from Old English (the widely known "The Seafarer"), Middle English, Greek, Latin, Provençal, Chinese, and Japanese. In all of them he combined a lively modernity and respect for the spirit of the original. For example, he offered this passage in his *Homage to Sextus Propertius*:

We have kept our erasers in order,
A new-fangled chariot follows the flower-hung horses;
A young Muse with young loves clustered about her
ascends with me into the aether, . . .
And there is no high-road to the Muses.[3]

He sought to make his translations both true and new by approaching the task creatively. Hugh Kenner writes about Pound: "Translating does not, for him, differ in essence from any other poetic job; as the poet begins by seeing, so the translator by reading; but his reading must be a kind of seeing."[4] R. P. Blackmur reinforces this observation by writing of *Homage to Sextus*

Propertius: "We know that this Homage is a portrait not a photograph, the voice a new recital not a dictaphone record. We know, in short, that Mr. Pound begins his work where ordinary translators leave off—with a reduction of English and Latin fractions to a common denominator; he proceeds to a new work built up from that denominator."[5]

Following these guidelines, H. D. achieved significant results. In 1916, she published *Choruses from Iphigenia in Aulis*; three years later, these were reprinted, along with several choruses from Euripides' *Hippolytus.* Both translations, together with what she called "choruses" from the *Odyssey* (actually the opening of the epic as far as Athena's plea that Zeus allow Odysseus to leave Calypso), were included in *Collected Poems* (1925). In *Red Roses for Bronze* (1931), there are three lengthy translations: "Choros Translations (from The *Bacchae*)," "Sea-Choros (from *Hecuba*)," and "Choros Sequence (from *Morpheus*)." Her most ambitious work was published in 1937—*Euripides' Ion, Translated with Notes.*[6]

A reader unskilled in Latin and Greek is limited to reporting his impression of these translations and the opinions of more competent judges. From this standpoint, it is obvious that H. D.'s translations from Greek drama resemble her original lyrics. By rendering the verse in her typical manner—short, staccato lines of free verse, arranged in units of intense speech—and by choosing passages that express her customary themes, she completely naturalizes her sources. In fact, if she had not acknowledged the original texts, a reader would easily accept these translations as original work.

For example, a passage from the chorus of the women of Chalkis in *Iphigenia in Aulis* reminds the reader of the manner, mood, and imagery of several of H. D.'s poems:

> If a god should stand here
> He could not speak
> At the sight of ships
> Circled with ships.
>
> This beauty is too much
> For any woman.
> It is burnt across my eyes.
>
> (*Collected Poems*, p. 108)

Her expression of the unbearable intensity of beauty brings to mind the first stanza of her widely known lyric "Orchard":

> I saw the first pear
> as it fell—
> the honey-seeking, golden-banded,
> the yellow swarm
> was not more fleet than I,
> (spare us from loveliness)
> and I fell prostrate
> crying:
> you have flayed us
> with your blossoms,
> spare us the beauty
> of fruit-trees.
>
> (*Collected Poems*, p. 40)

Similarly, in *Hippolytus*, Phaedra's wish for the ecstasy of the hunt is in harmony with many of H. D.'s outcries for dangerous adventure. Phaedra says:

> Take me to the mountains!
> O for woods, pine tracts,
> where hounds athirst for death,
> leap on the bright stags!
> God, how I would shout to the beasts
> with my gold hair torn loose;
> I would shake the Thessalian dart,
> I would hurl the barbed arrow from my grasp.
>
> (*Collected Poems*, p. 128)

In "Huntress," H. D. writes:

> Come, blunt your spear with us,
> our pace is hot
> and our bare heels
> in the heel-prints—
> we stand tense—do you see—
> are you already beaten
> by the chase?
>
> (*Collected Poems*, p. 32)

The most important reaction to these fragmentary translations was expressed by T. S. Eliot in an essay, "Euripides and Professor Murray," written in 1920. Eliot favorably compared H. D.'s rendering of the *Iphigenia in Aulis* and *Hippolytus* to Murray's translations. Eliot's purpose clearly was to attack Murray, and H. D. gained by serving as a foil:

> Greek poetry will never have the slightest vitalizing effect upon English poetry if it can only appear masquerading as a vulgar debasement of the eminently personal idiom of Swinburne. . . . This is really a point of capital importance. That the most conspicuous Greek propagandist of the day should almost habitually use two words where the Greek language requires one, and where the English language will provide him with one; . . . that he should stretch the Greek brevity to fit the loose frame of William Morris, and blur the Greek lyric to the fluid haze of Swinburne; these are not faults of infinitesimal insignificance.[7]

Eliot concluded by remarking that "as a poet, Mr. Murray is merely a very insignificant follower of the pre-Raphaelite movement."[8]

Eliot saw H. D.'s translations as a sign that Greek literature was passing into the guardianship of more competent poets. Recognizing that she had accomplished little as yet, his praise for her was as cautious as his dismissal of Murray was sharp. Nevertheless, he found her translations promising, if not expert:

> The choruses from Euripides by H. D. are, allowing for errors and even occasional omissions of difficult passages, much nearer to both Greek and English than Mr. Murray's. But H. D. and the other poets of the "Poets' Translation Series" have so far done no more than pick up some of the more romantic crumbs of Greek literature; none of them has yet shown himself competent to attack the *Agamemnon.*[9]

More enthusiastic but vague praise was given to H. D. by the classical scholar, Henry Rushton Fairclough. In 1926, his presidential address to the American Philological Association was entitled "The Classics and Our Twentieth-Century Poets." He restricted himself to American poets and singled out Edwin Arlington Robinson and H. D. as "the two greatest American poets now living."[10] His admiration for H. D. was boundless; he told his audience that "she has completely transported herself into the Hellenic past, or (shall we say?) that she has made ancient Hellas live again in the present."[11] Placing his professional position in the service of her praise, he stated: "Indeed, a Greek scholar, after a perusal of her work, cannot but conclude that in Greek poetry and art H. D. lives and moves and has her being. So completely is she suffused with the Greek spirit that only the use of the vernacular will often remind the cultivated reader that he is not reading a Greek poet."[12]

Unfortunately, Fairclough's remarks about the translations in *Collected Poems* were either pedantic or general. He described their style as "*staccato*, strikingly plain and direct, and the sentence-structure paratactic";[13] but he made no comment about the appropriateness of this style to the originals, except to say that the translations, like all her other work, were beautiful. Obviously, he was so taken with the Grecian spirit of her poems that he could not bring himself to examine them with a critic's eye. In fact, he charmingly excused himself from judging a writer in whom he took such delight: "Of the many eulogies passed upon H. D. there are some which I am tempted to cite, because I can hardly trust my own enthusiasm for her."[14]

A far different reaction was offered by Douglas Bush, who surveyed all of H. D.'s translations except *Ion*, as well as her original work written prior to 1937. He found Eliot "somewhat unkind to Mr. Murray and more than kind to H. D."[15] He also raised a point that her *Ion* would later help to settle: he stated that although Murray's Swinburnean style was indeed objectionable, he felt no optimism about the prospect of an entire play done in H. D.'s manner. He feared that it would be still "less readable and probably even less Greek" than Murray's; moreover, he added parenthetically, "one shudders at the thought of the *Odyssey* done in the staccato strut of H. D.'s 'chorus' specimen."[16]

The heart of his censure was that H. D. is untrue to her originals. He claimed that "alterations of detail are everywhere."[17] The early translations struck him as hectic; the passages from the *Bacchae* and *Hecuba* in *Red Roses for Bronze* seemed "less bright and rocky and stiff than the earlier experiments, and more verbose—the one chorus from *Hecuba* has a hundred and thirty words in Greek and four hundred and fifty in English."[18] The greatest compliment he permitted himself to pay her was that "H. D. is generally superior to Mr. Murray in salience, energy, and speed, yet the two come together when they find an occasion to turn simple, concrete, human sentiments into an eighteen-ninetyish cult of Beauty."[19] His final remark reinforces the impression that he not only found her translations wanting but that her poetic manner displeased him: "the translations produced almost exactly the same effect as many of H. D.'s original poems, and if there is one thing certain in the realm of poetry it is that Euripides was not like H. D."[20]

The one translation that Douglas Bush was not able to consider is, of course, her most important—Euripides' *Ion.* It is her only attempt to meet the challenge that both he and T. S. Eliot mentioned: the handling of an entire play. That she chose *Ion* for this venture is not surprising, for it presents a situation remarkably in accord with the themes of her verse. The sadness and pride of Kreousa, raped by Apollo and uncertain of the fate of her child, and the perplexity of Ion about his parentage and his relationship to Apollo, provide H. D. with an opportunity to deal as a translator with several themes important in her own work. The dangers of physical love, the suffering involved in placing oneself at the disposal of absolute forces—whether of love, art, or religion—and the ultimate glory of such a commitment are matters as important to H. D. as, in this play, to Euripides.

She accompanies her translation with significant comments—she calls them simply "the translator's personal interpretation" and adds that "the play may be read straight through" without considering them (ix). In these comments she presents her view of a translator's task as well as her judgment of the meaning of the drama. Her distaste for pedantry is reiterated, accompanied by the assertion that the direct experience of Greece is as effective a way of understanding Greek culture as studying the language:

> We may relegate the boy, Ion, to the dust-heap and parse his delicate phrases till we end in a mad-house. It will bring us no nearer to the core of Greek beauty. Parse the sun in heaven, distinguish between the taste of mountain air on different levels, feel with your bare foot a rock covered with sea-weed, one covered with sand, one washed and marbled by the tide. You cannot learn Greek, only, with a dictionary. You can learn it with your hands and your feet and especially with your lungs. (12)

In speaking of her handling of the initial dialogue between Ion and Kreousa, she admits that she has altered the form of the original: "The broken, exclamatory or evocative *vers-libre* which I have chosen to translate the two-line dialogue, throughout the play, is the exact antithesis of the original. Though concentrating and translating sometimes, ten words, with two, I have endeavoured, in no way, to depart from the meaning. There are just under a hundred of these perfectly matched statements, questions and answers. The original runs as sustained narrative" (32). This description of her style—"broken, exclamatory or evocative *vers-libre*"—applies in varying degrees to the entire translation. She does not explain how this admittedly sharp stylistic divergence from the original can be achieved without some alteration of Euripides' meaning.

H. D.'s notes also convey her understanding of the play. She begins by asking a rhetorical question: "Is this a worthy theme for great religious drama, the betrayal and desertion, by one of its most luminous figures, of a woman and her first child?" (6). Her answer is affirmative; although a "great English critic [undoubtedly Gilbert Murray] has used this play to point out forcibly the irony and rationalism of the mind of the poet" (9), she sees it differently. To her, it demonstrates the wisdom of yielding to God's commands, however imprudent it may seem. Although this yielding involves suffering, its outcome is ultimately joyful. By "God's commands"—the imperious will of Apollo in *Ion*—she seems to mean impulses justified not by practicality but by psychological and spiritual urgency. H. D. expresses this hopeful view in her comment upon the remarks of Pallas Athene at the end of the play:

> This most beautiful abstraction of antiquity and of all time, pleads for the great force of the under-mind or the unconscious that so often, on the point of blazing upward into the glory of inspirational creative thought, flares, by a sudden law of compensation, down, making for tragedy, disharmony, disruption, disintegration, but in the end, O, in the end, if we have patience to wait, she says, if we have penetration and faith and the desire actually to follow all those hidden subterranean forces, how great is our reward. (122)

Thus H. D. attributes a courageous idealism to Euripides that is far unlike the scepticism often found in his work.

Ion was reviewed by Richard Lattimore, one of the most distinguished contemporary translators of classical Greek.[21] Generally, his remarks were in accord with Douglas Bush's evaluation of her earlier translations. Although Lattimore seemed to take greater pleasure than Bush in H. D.'s personal style, he protested that she distorts Euripides' language and tone. He took exception particularly to her handling of the first recognition scene between Ion and Xouthos (53): "The Greek is written in trochaic tetrameter (the metre of *Locksley Hall*) clear, brisk, unequivocal; the translation is confused and feverish." He then gave examples of H. D.'s disjointed dialogue and concluded: "But actually, Ion and Xouthos were talking in sentences; and what Ion said was, literally, 'Stand back, before you get an arrow through your lungs.' "[22]

The heart of Lattimore's criticism was that "H. D. (and others have done this) seems to treat Euripides as if he were only, or always, a lyrist. He was far more."[23] In H. D.'s version, Lattimore missed Euripides' narration and elucidation, the passages that show him as "a debater, a propagandist, and a moralist; one who was aware of sex hatreds and class hatreds; one who did not mince or veil his words."[24] He found that her notes express the same attenuation. Granting that she "has based on the original a dramatic poem with much beauty in it"[25] but objecting that "Euripides was not in an ecstasy all the time, or even most of it"[26] and that it is indefensible to treat "Greek tragedy as a sustained lyric,"[27] he categorized the translation as a "pseudomorph."[28]

II Hippolytus Temporizes

H. D.'s most important adaptation of a classical text is her three-act play, *Hippolytus Temporizes*.[29] Although based upon Euripides' *Hippolytus*, it contains significant innovations in plot and theme. H. D. employs the dangerous strategy of using an established work as the foundation for one of her own.

Generally, she was successful at this type of venture. In this case, it enabled her to extend her essentially lyrical talent to the dimensions of drama. By choosing a traditional tale, she could count on the reader's prior awareness of action that she would have had difficulty dramatizing. She used Euripides' play as she used autobiography in her prose fiction but with the advantage that Euripides' work is better known than her life. She faced the likelihood, of course, that her play would suffer by comparison with his, but she probably felt that this was a small risk to take for the chance to write a tragedy.

Doing an adaptation also made irrelevant the objections expressed by Bush and Lattimore against her translations of *Hippolytus, Iphigenia in Aulis*, and *Ion.* In an adaptation, changes from the original in mood and action are expected, and differences in versification are entirely at the will of the author. The obligations of the translator are the options of the adaptor; innovations are virtually required. This condition favors an artist like H. D., who had a strong creative will, a weak talent for narration, and a lively responsiveness to the classics.

Choosing the Hippolytus story was equally promising. She had already shown her devotion to Euripides' play by translating portions of it. She had also paid tribute to it in her novel *Hedylus.* When Hedylus is asked by his mother, "'Poems by moonlight? . . . Were you scanning the great lines of Euripides?' he replies, 'You guessed right. . . . The metres of the huntsman Hippolytus hanging offerings to his goddess.' . . . Euripides. Hippolytus. Worn metres that held silver as the moon her radiance. The choruses were crescent-shaped, horn-tipped, tenuous, and inevitable as the shafts of that same Artemis" (40). Moreover, the tale of Hippolytus is the subject of four lyrics included in *Collected Poems*: "Hippolytus Temporizes" (printed as a prefatory poem to the play), "Phaedra," "She Contrasts with Herself Hippolyta," and "She Rebukes Hippolyta."

H. D. used the Hippolytus story to dramatize conflicts between chastity and sexuality and, more subtly, between spiritual and physical love. This survey of her poems and novels has already shown how central to her work these conflicts are. Her sensibility was principally attuned to the tensions of love. For such a poetic temperament, the Hippolytus story is particularly congenial. She saw it as a classical representation of perennially meaningful themes. Basing her play upon it enabled her to merge personal concerns within a well-known narrative.

Two prefatory pieces deserve notice—"The Argument" and the previously mentioned lyric "Hippolytus Temporizes" (probably this poem was the seed of the play). "The Argument" outlines the play and serves as both an enticement and a compensation for any deficiency in narration. It also suggests how H. D. diverges from Euripides:

> This is the familiar story of Theseus of Athens. Hippolytus, his son and the child of Hippolyta, inflames a later wife, the Cretan princess, Phaedra, in her palace outside Troezen in Attica.

> Theseus, King of Athens, finds his rival in his own son, the stepson of his foreign queen.
>
> How Hippolytus returns the affection so secretly and tragically bestowed has become a legend, the prototype of unrequited passion for many centuries. Hippolytus is his mother again, frozen lover of the forest which maintains personal form for him in the ever-present vision, yea, even the bodily presence of the goddess Artemis.
>
> Phaedra by a trick (as we see in the second act of this play) gains the passion of the youth. The boy, as tradition has always maintained, in a frenzied drive along an infuriated seacoast, is broken and mercilessly battered by the waves. The consequence of his death to two of the Olympians is here set forth in the final act of this tragedy, *Hippolytus Temporizes.*

In this version, Hippolytus is intimate with Phaedra, although "by a trick" on her part, and Theseus remains ignorant of their relationship. In fact, Theseus is referred to merely as Phaedra's aged and unsatisfactory lover; he does not even appear. As a consequence of the reduction of his role, the significance of Hippolytus' death is changed. As in Euripides' play, he is fatally injured while driving his chariot, but here the meaning of his fate—whether or not life is well lost for love—is debated by three Olympians—Artemis, Helios, and Eros.

Regrettably, the prefatory poem "Hippoltyus Temporizes" suggests a misleading view of Hippolytus' relationship with Phaedra. It is a dramatic monologue in which Hippolytus prays to his beloved Artemis. Each stanza opens with some variation upon the line "I worship the greatest first," but it is followed by a parenthetical expression of love for Phaedra. The implication is that he is actually in love with his stepmother, but that perhaps, because the relationship is illicit, he has transferred his passion to the goddess. This suggestion is interesting but irrelevant, because in the play Hippolytus gives no sign that he is in love with Phaedra; indeed, she resorts to a trick because she knows that only by deception can her passion be satisfied.

The play centers upon the different kinds of happiness sought by Artemis, Hippolytus, and Phaedra. Artemis wishes to become a pure spirit, not merely a goddess. Not only is she affronted by sensual behavior; even chaste devotion annoys her. She begins and ends the play by expressing a desire to hide from mankind in the fastnesses of nature:

> I heard the intolerable rhythm
> and sound of prayer,
> so I have hidden
> where no mortals are,
> no sycophant of priest
> to mar my ease,
> climbing impassible stairs
> of rock
> and forest shale
> and barriers of trees:
>
> someone will come
> after I shun this place
> and set up a circle,
> blunt end up,
> of stones,
> flattened and hewn,
> and pile an altar,
> but I shall have gone further (1)

She wishes to enjoy nature without being limited in any way by its laws. Her ecstasies are solitary and cold; significantly, her retinue consists of the souls of youths who died before experiencing love. She expects adoration but prefers to receive it from innocent ghosts rather than from living worshippers.

Unlike Artemis, Hippolytus is a lover, but he wants no mortal partner. The thought of an ordinary love affair repels him because he yearns for union with Artemis herself. Only the self-sufficient goddess of chastity arouses his passion. Yet his attitude toward her is ambiguous. Although at times he speaks like a lover—"hot, hot, is my desire/to trace you in the forest" (15)—elsewhere he seems eager for death: "I would only rest/forgetting everything/in this cold place" (19). Once he even calls Artemis "Mother," but she quickly disavows this role. These conflicting impulses are never reconciled, but they do suggest motives for his extraordinary infatuation.

In contrast, Phaedra seeks an earthly lover. She is presented as despising the idealism of the Greeks, so alien to the more sensual outlook of her native Crete:

O how I hate
this world, this west, this power
that strives to reach
through river, town or flower,
the god or spirit that inhabits it;
O, is it not enough to greet
the red-rose
for the red, red sweet of it?
must we encounter
with each separate flower,
some god, some goddess? (44)

Phaedra's general discontent with Greece is intensified by her unhappy personal life. She is married to the noble but aged Theseus who, in her opinion, offers only "the dotard love/of a dull king" (45). The presence of Hippolytus, her stepson, makes an agony of her lonesomeness. She finds his beauty irresistible, but he is aloof and indifferent toward her. She is frustrated into boldness by his continually roaming the forests in search of Artemis.

The action springs from their conflicting desires. The setting is: "Below Troezen. A wild gorge or ravine cuts through the trees on to a flat sandy beach." There Hippolytus discovers the fugitive Artemis, whom he has long been seeking, but he is ordered by the goddess to stop pursuing her. She resents his attentions; moreover, she reminds him that his destiny is to rule Athens. Hippolytus says that he hates court life and that she alone in all the world attracts him. The goddess then refers disdainfully—but also jealously—to Phaedra. When Hippolytus pities his "dotard sire, . . . captured father," Artemis warns him to "beware the capturer/who may snare another" (10). She adds portentously, "I am told charms call you/to her favour." Although he insists, "Not I—not I—I am no wanton's lover," Artemis warns him, "I do not stay to rival/anyone" (14).

After Artemis departs, the courtier Hyperides arrives to persuade Hippolytus to abandon his anti-social behavior: "have done/with all this murky game,/. . ./demand your place in life,/your share in power/and social intercourse" (28). Hippolytus denounces him as a "courtly bore" and "tiresome young idiot" (38) and gets rid of him and his companions by ordering them back to the court to prepare a woodland festival for Artemis. After they leave, Hippolytus lies down on a cloak provided by a mysterious boy who says he has just been shipwrecked on a vessel from Cyprus. Hippolytus falls asleep, sighing for Artemis.

The second act takes place nearby on the same strip of sea-coast. Phaedra and her retinue arrive. Although the beach is consecrated to Artemis, Phaedra boldly speaks of her passion for Hippolytus and implores Aphrodite to satisfy her desire. When the boy who provided the cloak for Hippolytus appears, she indulges the fancy that he is Eros and that her prayer has been heard. She then sends the boy to tell Hippolytus that Artemis has at last yielded to his importunity and wishes to become his lover:

> tell to your lord,
> your prince Hippolytus
> that Artemis chooses
> actually as a goddess,
> love, love, love, love
> that mocks the lure of forests,
> love that enchants the sea-fowl and the beast. (64-65)

When the boy leaves, Phaedra commands her servants to construct a pavilion. In a short while, the boy returns to announce that Hippolytus is coming.

The next scene takes place at the same spot several hours later. Phaedra emerges from the tent in an ecstasy of sensual delight. Her maid urges her to flee Artemis' precinct, but Phaedra wildly declares: "I have made it mine,/have made it Love's" (71). However, her happiness is brief, for Hippolytus appears, also in ecstasy about his amorous encounter but convinced that he has been intimate with Artemis. Phaedra's subterfuge has succeeded only too well; when Hippolytus notices her, he accuses her of violating Artemis' sanctuary. She tries to lead him to accept the truth by telling him that she has just enjoyed an intimacy as intense as his; she promises him that, like many men, he will find "a goddess in a woman's arms" (75). He denies the possibility and pledges himself to Artemis forever. His repudiation of Phaedra is so sharp that she enters the pavilion in despair. As Hippolytus loses himself in his morning prayer to the goddess, Phaedra's dying moans are heard.

In the next scene, several hours have elapsed, and Hippolytus is still absorbed in prayer. The tent has been removed, and Hyperides arrives to announce that Phaedra has committed suicide. When Hippolytus eargerly tells him about his intimacy with

Artemis, Hyperides, realizing what has occurred, bluntly tells him that he has slept with Phaedra. However, the truth makes no impression upon Hippolytus, and he decides upon a fatal gesture of triumph: "Call me my steeds,/is there a mortal yet/arises/after resting with a goddess,/other than wild and passionate and glad" (94).

In the final act, Hippolytus has been flung from his chariot and lies at the base of a statue of Artemis. When he repeatedly implores the goddess to help him, the god Helios (H. D.'s customary name for Apollo) appears, wondering why Artemis ignores the plea of a devoted and fatally stricken worshipper. Finally she arrives and rebukes them both: "Silence then both of you/with your indictments/and your tyrannies,/how can you judge the true,/the upright,/righteous/or the holy man?" (103). She complains that she has been insulted. As though to underscore her complaint, the dying Hippolytus speaks fervidly of the intimacy he believes he has shared with her. The boy then enters, singing love's praises. When Artemis points to the mutilated body of Hippolytus as an example of the destructiveness of love, the boy—virtually confirming his identity as Eros—contends that Hippolytus' injuries are his glory. A brief debate establishes the absolute irreconcilability of their views:

ARTEMIS: His heart is taken
and his soul is gone—
BOY: His hands and side
blossom with holy wound—
ARTEMIS: His soul and body
are broken and defamed—
BOY: His soul is beautiful
in Love's great name—
ARTEMIS: His body pallid,
wan and without fame—
BOY: His body bright
with red and luminous blood—
ARTEMIS: His body is disgraced
by treacherous love—
BOY: His body blossoms
as Adonis did
ARTEMIS: He has no place now
in my sacred grove—
BOY: He shows more holy
for the strain of love— (112-13)

After Hippolytus dies, Helios takes up the defense of love. Although he concedes that "Eros is still man's tyrant/and god's king" (116), this truth does not distress him. In fact, when a chorus of Artemis' ghostly maidens appears, chanting of the joy of lovelessness, he dismisses them sharply: "Nay/nay/be gone,/I feel the web,/the ecstasy, the lure/of peace,/the power/that negates life,/be off/I see,/I see/the snare" (122). He rejects Artemis' behavior as hostile to life; he prefers love at any cost, although he laments the high toll it usually exacts.

Helios wishes to restore Hippolytus to life, despite the opposition of Artemis, who prefers to make him a revered symbol of love's suffering, like Hyacinth. Her allusion to Hyacinth moves Helios ruefully to protest that Hyacinth, reduced to a mere flower, "was chill/and it was cold/and O no bitterness/can equal that keen sorrow/that I had" (128). She insists that she would keep Hippolytus "sacred and apart,/and I would have him/chill against my heart" (128). The issue between them is whether love is to be a living experience or an abstraction.

Helios prevails and restores Hippolytus to life. However, the revived youth is still ecstatic over his supposed intimacy with Artemis. The goddess, shocked by his sensuality, orders him back to death. This time, Helios accepts her wish, remarking sadly that once again he has been unable to spare the life of a young lover. The play ends as Artemis renews her determination to flee deep into the forest "where no mortals are."

Except for the diminution of Theseus, H. D. keeps to the main issue of Euripides' tragedy, even though she alters the plot. Both plays emphasize the tension between physical and platonic love. Moreover, both appear to reach the same recognition, though by different routes, that human beings cannot ignore their physical nature. Although the desire to transcend physical limitations by giving one's love to a pure spirit is presented sympathetically, both plays depict its fatal consequences.

Euripides establishes this theme simply: he allows Aphrodite to punish Hippolytus for spurning the rites of physical love. By presenting human traits as jealous deities, Euripides clearly suggests that men must respect the conditions of human nature. H. D. expresses herself obliquely. Her manner is vivid but her meaning is often uncertain; her characters tend to declaim rather than converse. As R. P. Blackmur has written, many of their utterances, "while 'thrilling,' are bastard and have no posterity in the mind."[30] Nonetheless, H. D.'s outlook is clearly congruent with Euripides': both find Hippolytus' and Artemis' behavior unacceptable.

These conclusions arise from a knot of ironic relationships. In desiring to love Artemis, Hippolytus represents not chastity but exalted erotic ambition, as proved by his vulnerability to Phaedra's trick. Because he never realizes how he has been tricked, he causes Phaedra to commit suicide and Artemis to be disgusted by his sensuality. His fatal chariot ride is prompted by his ecstasy at having not only worshipped a goddess but made love to her. He is more likable than Euripides' protagonist because he is less virginal, but also he is the more surely doomed. The intervention of Theseus and Poseidon is not needed to bring about his death; he destroys himself by seeking to enjoy earthly pleasures with a goddess.

Hippolytus' plight also reveals the limitations of Artemis' behavior. Her wish to be free from personal attachments is beguiling and may be proper for deities but, as the entire play shows, inappropriate for human beings. Moreover, her desire for independence is compromised by her unwillingness to be totally self-sufficient. She wants worshippers, but she wishes them to make no demands upon her. H. D. aptly dramatizes the incongruity of this desire by having Artemis served by virgin ghosts.

H. D.'s handling of these complex attitudes is impressive. In recognizing both the appeal and the folly of Hippolytus and Artemis, she reaches the level of tragedy. No facile solutions are ventured; she acknowledges the nobility of idealism, but she also indicates how easily high-mindedness may lead to a self-destructive escapism.

This viewpoint demonstrates a maturing of H. D.'s understanding. In her earlier work, the negative tendencies expressed by Artemis and Hippolytus receive considerable approval. In *Hippolytus Temporizes*, the limitations of human love are still recognized, but the alternative is seen to be even less feasible. H. D. sees that although to love another person is no assurance of ideal fulfillment, it at least avoids emotional sterility and gross self-deception. For Hippolytus to love Phaedra, even if she were not married, would involve difficulties, but it would not be so dangerous as pursuing an unwilling goddess or pretending that a mortal woman is divine.

CHAPTER 6

The Impact of World War II

AFTER the publication in 1937 of the translation of Euripides' *Ion*, H. D. did not bring out another volume until 1944. The intervening years were spent mostly in a struggle for survival, for she lived in London during World War II. She shared the hardships of the English people and experienced with them the tremendous joy of victory. As the life of the nation was renewed, she felt an intense revival of her spiritual faith. Looking back, she came to believe that the five years' ordeal had cleansed and strengthened her soul.

The tensions of this ordeal dominate the five volumes that she wrote from 1942 to 1946, but which were published over a much longer span of years. There was a trilogy of war poems: *The Walls Do Not Fall,*[1] written in 1942 and published in 1944; *Tribute to the Angels,*[2] written in 1944 and published in 1945; and *The Flowering of the Rod,*[3] also composed in 1944 but not appearing until 1946. *By Avon River,*[4] her celebration of Shakespeare and other stout-spirited English writers of the Renaissance, was completed in 1946, although not published until 1949; and her *Tribute to Freud,*[5] written in 1944, was not published until 1956. In all these works, H. D. seeks to comprehend violence and to sustain her belief in a benevolent divine spirit.

I Tribute to Freud

Of these volumes, *Tribute to Freud* is the most appropriate to discuss first. It is an account of H. D.'s psychoanalysis with Freud in the 1930's. In the spring of 1933, for more than three months, she had daily sessions at Freud's home in Vienna. Then she left the city but returned in the fall of the following year and resumed the analysis for five weeks. Ten years later, as the war was drawing to a close, she wrote about her relationship with the famous doctor.

Naturally, the book has received most attention as an impression of Freud—one of many reminiscences by his patients. Indeed, Freud's biographer Ernest Jones has commended it highly. He is careful to emphasize that H. D. offers an appreciation rather than a biography, but the pleasure he takes in it is unmistakable:

> The book, with its appropriate title, is surely the most delightful and precious appreciation of Freud's personality that is ever likely to be written. Only a fine creative artist could have written it. It is like a lovely flower, and the crude pen of a scientist hesitates to profane it by attempting to describe it. I can only say that I envy anyone who has not yet read it, and that it will live as the most enchanting ornament of all the Freudian biographical literature.[6]

More pertinent here is its revelation of H. D.'s beliefs. Essentially the work is a self-portrait brought into focus by her confrontation with Freud. Her remarks express her state of mind in 1944 as she looked back upon an experience that had occurred ten years earlier.

Although readers may find the book self-conscious, loosely organized, and either sentimental or conceited, the counterbalance to these drawbacks is its ingenuous candor. H. D. says that she began the analysis in order "to dig down and dig out, root out my personal weeds, strengthen my purpose, reaffirm my beliefs, canalize my energies" (138). There may have been more specific problems requiring psychiatric attention, but, as she recounts the experience, the heart of her relationship with Freud was the issue of immortality. She sought help in overcoming doubts about the timeless life of the soul.

She had been attracted to Freud because he emphasized the importance of dreams and had achieved considerable success in understanding them. Her warmest praise is given to his accomplishment in this area:

> He had dared to say that the dream came from an unexplored depth in man's consciousness and that this unexplored depth ran like a great stream or ocean underground, and the vast depth of that ocean was the same vast depth that today, as in Joseph's day, overflowing in man's small consciousness, produced inspiration, madness, creative idea or the dregs of the dreariest symptoms of mental unrest and disease. He had dared to say that it was the same ocean of universal consciousness, and even if not stated in so many words, he had dared to imply that this consciousness

> proclaimed all men one; all nations and races met in the universal world of the dream; and he had dared to say that the dream-symbol could be interpreted; its language, its imagery were common to the whole race, not only of the living but of those ten thousand years dead. The picture-writing, the hieroglyph of the dream, was the common property of the whole race; in the dream, man, as at the beginning of time, spoke a universal language, and man, meeting in the universal understanding of the unconscious or the subconscious, would forgo barriers of time and space, and man, understanding man, would save mankind. (107-8)

She was fascinated by the hypothesis that dreams are a timeless language bridging cultures and ages, for she had a similar belief about classical mythology. That Freud actually recognized mythic patterns in dreams seemed to confirm her strongest surmise. Her hope was that he would teach her to recognize messages about immortality in the "hieroglyphic of the unconsciousness" (141).

H. D.'s cultural heritage and personal disposition both supported her faith in the immortality of the soul. She had always assumed the "soul's existence in some form or other, after it has shed the outworn or outgrown body" (64), and the many discouragements to idealism that she had experienced only gave a greater urgency to this belief. Her longing for the Absolute endured despite, and partly because of, the unhappiness of her life. She clung to the faith that the shortcomings of time would be overcome in eternity.

The roadblock in her psychoanalysis was that Freud did not share her faith. As she expressed it: "About the greater transcendental issues, we never argued. But there was an argument implicit in our very bones" (16). She knew that to him "belief in the soul's survival, in a life after death . . . was the last and greatest phantasy, the gigantic wish-fulfillment that had built up, through the ages, the elaborate and detailed picture of an after-life" (156). More troubling was the recognition that Freud "had no idea—it seemed impossible—really no idea that he would 'wake up' when he shed the frail locust-husk of his years, and find himself alive" (63). She was disappointed to observe that "his concern for immortality was translated into terms of grandchildren" (94).

H. D. tried to reconcile their differences by attributing to

Freud a wise prudence. She conceded that peoples' notions of immortality are usually only projections of the unconscious wishes and fears of their personal lives. From this tangle, little objectivity can be expected, either about human or supernatural affairs. She saw that Freud's concentration upon personal, mundane involvements offered the advantage of clearing up an undergrowth that would necessarily compromise any speculation about the soul. "Until we have completed our 12 labours, he seemed to reiterate, we (mankind) have no right to rest on cloud-cushion phantasies and dreams of an after-life" (157). She even attributed to his naturalism a therapeutic value compatible with her beliefs by conceding that since mankind "had profited so little by the illuminating teaching of the Master who gave his name to our present era, that it was well for a Prophet, in the old tradition of Israel, to arise, to slam the door on visions of the future, of the afterlife" (155).

Despite H. D.'s good-willed and sensible effort to understand Freud's outlook, the distance between them is obvious. She cherished a religious sensibility, and he was suspicious of it. They met on the common ground of psychology, but her inclination was always to transcend natural causes. She wanted to untangle the strands of her personal life, but she believed that an essential thread was her involvement in a spiritual plane of existence. While Freud saw this belief as phantasy, she regarded it as fact and sought to liberate this transcendent truth from personal complications. Freud's assumption was that analysis would exorcise her from an illusion; hers was that it would enable her to realize her immortal destiny more consciously. This divergence is apparent also in their attitude toward symbols. They both found ancient myths and archetypal images fascinating—H. D. says that Freud took pleasure in showing her his collection of ancient Greek, Egyptian, and Oriental figurines (102). However, she saw them as signatures of immortality, whereas to him they were the esthetic expression of anxiety and desire.

Consequently, H. D.'s book is both a tribute to Freud and a disavowal of his naturalistic viewpoint. This two-sided attitude accounts for the presence of both admiring and condescending remarks about him. If her faith in immortality was wavering at the time of her analysis, it was firm at the time she wrote this account. She conveys a confidence in the invincible and transcendent human spirit—the same kind of confidence that she expressed in the trilogy of war poems written about the same time. She is able to look back upon her experience with Freud with respect and affection that apparently were mutual and with a spiritual optimism that he gave no sign of sharing. Ten years after her visits to him, she recalls his ancient art treasures and asserts that even then she "knew the things in his room were symbols of Eternity and contained him then, as Eternity contains him now" (154).

II *The War Trilogy*

The three volumes—*The Walls Do Not Fall, Tribute to the Angels,* and *The Flowering of the Rod*—were H. D.'s first books of verse since *Red Roses for Bronze* in 1931, and they show a considerable change in her style. Instead of indeterminate stanzas of free verse, characterized by short lines and frequent reiteration, these poems are arranged in free verse couplets. The two-line unit gives an impression of regularity and uniformity not found in her earlier work. These poems also contain an innovation in diction: H. D. offers with apparent seriousness many elaborate and fantastic examples of word-play. To suggest the unity and continuity of certain mythological and religious concepts, she creates etymologies based upon a free-association of sound and concept. Amen, the Egyptian god, is linked to the epithet "Amen" in Christian prayers. Venus is associated with "venerate" and "Venice" but dissociated from "venery." In a play of opposites, *marah* (bitter) is joined to "Mary" and "myrrh." This practice, resembling a game of phonics controlled only by the demands of the theme, is more likely to strike the reader as silly than stimulating. In imagery, too, there is a difference between these volumes and the earlier ones. These poems seldom refer to classical Greece but often to ancient Egypt, the Bible, and hermetic writings. She seems to be broadening the scope of her religious references in order to include both the Semitic cultures of the Near East and Christianity. This shift is a consequence of her wish to establish the essential harmony of all religions, regardless of sectarian differences. In her earlier work she sought to escape from middle-class Christianity to an idealized Hellenism, but now she returns to a Christianity brought into union with the occult doctrines she believes to underlie all religions.

This trilogy has aptly been called "war poetry." It was written during the war, and its aim is to testify that war and faith in God are compatible and that the ordeal of war may even strengthen one's spiritual convictions. H. D.'s tone is far more hortatory than in her previous work. Undoubtedly these poems satisfied a creative impulse and contributed to her own serenity, but above all they manifest a didactic purpose. In fact, they are open to the charge that spiritual fervor pushed H. D. beyond the boundary of art. At times her utterances are commonplace, as though she assumed that the significance they bore for herself would be conveyed automatically to the reader. This assumption, dangerous for the missionary, is generally fatal for the artist.

The Walls Do Not Fall

The Walls Do Not Fall expresses H. D.'s idealism in the midst of war-devastated London. She contends that, despite the war, the spirit of man remains in union with God: "inspiration stalks us/through gloom://unaware, Spirit announces the Presence" (7). She neither questions the existence of this divine Spirit nor does she define its nature; her only concern is to assert that violence is in no way incompatible with the providence of God. By explaining how she has reached and sustained this conviction, she hopes to encourage others to do likewise. In this context, she sees the ability of the walls of some buildings to withstand repeated bombing as a metaphor for the strength of men to endure suffering in their search for God. To her fellow survivors, she asks the question: "we passed the flame: we wonder/what saved us? what for?" (8).

She declares that the mayhem wrought upon the city may intensify peoples' awareness of spiritual reality. The collapse of material civilization proves its impermanence and helps men to resist giving it their total allegiance. She also remarks upon the resemblance between the ruins of London and ancient sites, and she urges men to look for signs of perennial truth in the rubble just as they diligently explore ancient tombs in search of clues to the mystery of human consciousness: "let us search the old highways/for the true rune, the right spell,/recover old values" (9).

Her technique is to meditate upon the enduring significance of ancient images of the deity, such as Isis, Aset, and Astarte. She warns that this enterprise requires fortitude and cunning because people engaged in the war effort are certain to think her behavior decadent. However, like the mollusk, the seeker of religious truth must know when to protect himself from "the shark-jaws of outer circumstance" (12) by withdrawing into his shell, there to beget, perhaps, a "pearl-of-great-price" (12). Extending the image of the humble but invincible seeker, she calls herself a worm possessing no virtue except persistence:

> . . . I profit
> by every calamity;
>
> I eat my way out of it;
> gorged on vine-leaf and mulberry,
>
> parasite, I find nourishment:
> when you cry in disgust,
>
> a worm on the leaf,
> a worm in the dust,
>
> a worm on the ear-of-wheat,
> I am yet unrepentant,
>
> for I know how the Lord God
> is about to manifest, when I
>
> the industrious worm,
> spin my own shroud. (14-15)

She indicates the ironic place of the poet in modern society: people consider poets useless and pathetic, even though their contribution is now most needed. She asks her contemporaries, "If you do not even understand what words say,//how can you expect to pass judgement/on what words conceal?" (16). Poets, realizing that the secret of the gods "is stored/in man's very speech,//in the trivial or/the real dream" can provide guidance for an age thrust "back at the beginning" (16). Although the sword is dominant at the moment, "in the beginning/was the word" (18). Beyond all other men, poets have retained the power to hear the divine voice:

> we are the keepers of the secret,
> the carriers, the spinners
>
> of the rare intangible thread
> that binds all humanity

to ancient wisdom,
to antiquity;

our joy is unique, to us,
grape, knife, cup, wheat

are symbols in eternity,
and every concrete object

has abstract value, is timeless
in the dream parallel

whose relative sigil has not changed
since Nineveh and Babel. (23)

The life-giving message transmitted by poets is that the sun-god Amen must be reborn in man's consciousness: "He is the world-father" (23). Superficial religious practices must be purged, particularly the "pain-worship and death-symbol" of Christianity (25), for "*Amen* is our Christos" (26). In this remodeled Trinity, the Holy Ghost is the Dream—the channel of inspiration "open to everyone" (27):

it acts as go-between, interpreter,

it explains symbols of the past
in today's imagery,

it merges the distant future
with most distant antiquity,

states economically
in a simple dream-equation

the most profound philosophy. . . . (27)

H. D. reports that by meditating upon the image of the father-god and by associating him with the constellation Aries, the Ram, she has envisioned felicity. She desires to be a lamb snuggled in ram's wool or even to be consumed by the benevolent god: "let your teeth devour me,/let me be warm in your belly" (29). She wishes to be restored to the peace of nature and to enter into communion with the stars, the "personified messengers" of God (31).

She rejoices that her faith in God has survived personal griefs, but she admits that it has been shaken by the horrible incidents of the war—"I am hungry, the children cry for food/and flaming stones fall on them" (34). To overcome this condition, she has needed to feel the presence of God, as when Jesus comforted the apostles by preparing a meal for them some time after His resurrection. In the hope of gaining this reassurance, she has abandoned "sterile logic, trivial reason," and "dared occult lore" (36). She does not specify what "occult lore" means, but she admits that by following this route she has been "lost in sea-depth,//sub-conscious ocean where Fish/move two-ways, devour" (36). The result has been "a riot of unpruned imagination," "barren search," "illusion of lost-gods," and finally "*oneness lost, madness*" (37).

As an antidote to these dangerous byways, she dedicates herself "to spiritual realism" (40). She acknowledges the supremacy of God over the entire creation and recognizes that between Him and nature there is an infinite gulf. Yet she declares that everyone has his "personal approach/to the eternal realities" (44). Her way as a poet is to respond to "the meaning that words hide": "they are anagrams, cryptograms,/little boxes, conditioned//to hatch butterflies . . ." (44). She then demonstrates how she attempts to liberate the hidden meanings of words. Her technique is to play a spiritualistic word game whereby the sound and spelling of words with religious associations remind her of others of the same sort, regardless of the denotative gap between them. In this way, her consciousness of the oneness of the deity in all cultures is reinforced: "For example:/Osiris equates O-sir-is or O-sire-is;//Osiris,/the star Sirius, . ." (45). These pantheological associations give her the strength to continue seeking a closer realization of God. In the final passage of the poem, she reflects that just as some walls have withstood the bombing, some men carry on their spiritual pilgrimage despite harsh circumstances. She is proud to associate herself with these God-seekers:

> we are voyagers, discoverers
> of the not-known,
>
> the unrecorded;
> we have no map;
>
> possibly we will reach haven,
> heaven. (48)

Tribute to the Angels

Tribute to the Angels carries forward the meditation of *The Walls Do Not Fall*: the concluding lines of the first volume—"possibly we will reach haven,/heaven"—appear as a dedicatory epigraph to Osbert Sitwell in the second. The subject is still the tension between faith in God and the agony of war. H. D.'s approach to the subject remains eclectic; she refers to Hermes Trismegistus, the founder of occultism, as her patron and states that her ambition is to "melt down and integrate" (9) the precious stones of religious history that have been broken and scattered.

She is drawn particularly to the *Apocalypse* of St. John. Walls standing amid the ruins of London remind her of John's description of the imperishable walls of the New Jerusalem. Similarly, the unprecedented suffering caused by the war—"Never in Rome,/so many martyrs fell" (12)—suggests the ultimate cosmic battle of Armageddon. Continuing her reflection upon the *Apocalypse*, she is encouraged by the image of the seven archangels. She associates them with planetary spirits and accepts the fact that one, Uriel, governs war. This recognition leads her to the conclusion that war is part of the divine plan for the universe. She then begins to understand that war is an expression of the qualities of strength and courage that support mankind in crises; from this viewpoint, Uriel deserves as much respect as the other angels.

By playing her associative word game, she then transforms what had seemed like disaster into grounds for solace. Acting like an alchemist of language, she represents the troubles of the age by the Hebrew words *marah* and *mar* and places them in a crucible. Fire purges away all difficulties, leaving only a word of consolation:

> . . . *marah-mar*
> are melted, fuse and join
>
> and change and alter,
> mer, mere, mère, mater, Mais, Mary,
>
> Star of the Sea,
> Mother. (15)

H. D. claims that this "Mother" has also been known in other ages as Hesperus, Venus, Aphrodite, and Astarte. However, she emphasizes that the association of Venus and carnality is unjust: "knaves and fools/have done you impious wrong" (16-17). Apologizing to the goddess for such insults, she implores her assistance: "return, O holiest one,/Venus whose name is kin//to venerate/venerator" (17). The poet wishes to be sheltered by this divine mother whose benevolent presence she has realized as the fruit of her struggle with grief.

Her more serene mood is confirmed by the imagined voice of another angel, Annael—the peace of God. His gentleness deepens her awareness that war is a necessary but minor part of the cosmic harmony, like the concord of bells from Venetian campanili. By virtue of this realization, she is able even to revere the angel of war:

> So we hail them together,
> one to contrast the other,
>
> two of the seven Spirits,
> set before God
>
> as lamps on the high-altar,
> for one must inexorably
>
> take fire from the other (20-21)

The same truth is impressed upon her by reflecting upon the course of the seasons. Spring is sweeter after the bitterness of winter; after a season of dreadful violence in London, "never, never/was a season more beautiful" (21).

She then recounts two experiences that have strengthened her faith. The first is an actual occurrence. She had come upon a charred tree blossoming amid the rubble of a bombed-out building. The apparition had seemed like a miraculous vision:

> We are part of it;
> we admit the transubstantiation,
>
> not God merely in the bread
> but God in the other-half of the tree
>
> that looked dead—
> did I bow my head?
>
> did I weep? my eyes say,
> it was not a dream
>
> yet it was vision,
> it was a sign,

it was *the Angel which redeemed me,*
it was the Holy Ghost—

a half-burnt-out apple-tree
blossoming;

this is the flowering of the rood,
this is the flowering of the wood,

where Annael, we pause to give
thanks that we rise again from death and live. (25-26)

The second experience is literally a vision—and more affecting than the first. While thinking about the angel Michael, she had felt the presence of the divine Mother: "how could I imagine/ the Lady herself would come instead?" (29). The Lady, conveying a "cool beneficence" (31), was beautiful, dressed entirely in white; "the Child was not with her" (33). She showed a special concern for writers, "and she carried a book" (35) containing not ancient wisdom but "the unwritten volume of the new" (37). To H. D., she was unmistakably the loving Patroness of all truth-seekers: "She carried a book, either to imply/she was one of us, with us,//or to suggest she was satisfied/with our purpose, a tribute to the Angels" . . . (40).

By virtue of these reflections and visions, H. D. has liberated herself from bitterness; in its place she finds peace—"a cluster of garden-pinks/or a face like a Christmas-rose" (40). The poem ends with a repetition of her earlier celebration of this inner transformation: "*This is the flowering of the rod,/this is the flowering of the burnt-out wood,* . ." (42).

The Flowering of the Rod

The Flowering of the Rod is patterned like the other volumes of the trilogy, even to the use of the closing lines of the preceding volume as a dedicatory epigraph (in this case to Norman Holmes Pearson): "pause to give/thanks that we rise again from death and live." However, the theme is distinctly different. The first two volumes assert the possibility of believing in God at a time of unparalleled violence, but in *The Flowering of the Rod* this faith is assumed, as H. D. resolves to seek a mystical vision. Convinced of the omnipresence of a benevolent Spirit, she plans to turn her back on human affairs and to devote herself to achieving a transcendental union with God. Ordinary life is represented as shallow; she wishes to "mount higher/to love—resurrection" (8). Having outlasted the "bitter fire of destruction" (7), she plans to leave the world to its fate. She urges all god-seekers to do likewise: "leave the smouldering cities below/(we have done what we could)" (8).

Her attitude toward society is both defensive and condescending. She feels the need to explain her abandonment of "the world," but she does so by placing herself in the role of a rejected prophetess. She says that she has tried to offer mankind beauty, but her effort has been fruitless. In a time of war, men seek other satisfactions. She seems to have forgotten the view expressed in the preceding volume that war is part of a benign spiritual order; here, she sees war as an enemy to spiritual consciousness. She feels under no obligation to society; she "will go to the things I love" (8) and leave "the-place-of-a-skull/to those who have fashioned it" (9). She urges anyone who would join her to make a "simple affirmation" (9) for the higher life with no delay and no explanations—"does the first wild-goose stop to explain/to the others? no—he is off" (9). In order to bolster her confidence that "ultimately we will find//happiness," she reminds herself of the promise made by Jesus to the thief crucified beside him: "*today thou shalt be/with me in Paradise*" (10).

Clearly her desire is different from ordinary restlessness—the usual wish for a change from present circumstance. She wants nothing less than to experience eternity while still alive. She knows that failure in this endeavor is almost certain, but she believes that the sublimity of the goal gives dignity even to those who do not reach it:

> O, do not pity them, as you watch them drop one by one,
>
> for they fall exhausted, numb, blind
> but in certain ecstasy,
>
> for theirs is the hunger
> for Paradise. (12-13)

At least the lives of these seekers are oriented—they wish to follow "a bee-line/straight to the horde and plunder,/the treasure" (14); whereas most people find life a "foolish circling and senseless wheeling" with "no reason," "no vision" (13).

Rejoicing at the nobility of her quest, H. D. feels "*full of new wine*" and confident that she has "gone onward from bronze and iron,/into the Golden Age" (15). She insists that her transformation is "no poetic phantasy/but a biological reality,//a fact" (15), whose potency is so great that she warns others who are unwilling to venture on the same path:

> I live; I am alive;
>
> take care, do not know me,
> deny me, do not recognise me,
>
> shun me; for this reality
> is infectious—ecstasy. (16)

The paradigm for her effort is Jesus, whom she calls the first human being to achieve "resurrection." She believes that He continues to journey between heaven and earth so that men may benefit from His presence. His promise—"*today thou shalt be with me in Paradise*"—is relevant to all ages. Even though He made it to a man on the verge of death, H. D. takes it as a promise of a mystical experience. She notes particularly, also, that Jesus made this promise to a condemned criminal and that He showed a special fondness for Mary Magdalen, the fallen woman. These examples of benevolence toward outcasts encourage H. D. to be hopeful about the success of her quest:

> So the first—it is written,
> will be the twisted or the tortured individuals,
>
> out of line, out of step with world so-called progress;
> the first to receive the promise was a thief;
>
> the first actually to witness His life-after-death,
> was an unbalanced, neurotic woman (18-19)

In the remainder of the volume, H. D. narrates a similarly encouraging legend about Mary Magdalen. According to the legend, the balm that Mary used to anoint Jesus' feet was given to her by Kaspar, one of the Magi. Providentially, it was a matching jar to the one Kaspar had offered to the Infant at Bethlehem. This honor, bestowed upon a scandalous but loving woman, renews H. D.'s trust that her journey will also bring her to the embrace of God.

Summation

The "War Trilogy" illustrates the philosophic differences between H. D. and Freud. Preoccupied with the spiritual life, she regards the achievement of a mystical experience as supremely desirable and as worth any sacrifice. According to her account, Freud considered these attitudes the symptoms of anxiety. This difference of outlook accounts for her occasional condescension in *Tribute to Freud.*

Noteworthy, also, is her reduction of entire religions and complicated myths to belief in the benevolence of a divine mother and father, whose existence may be realized by all men but most readily by artists. In order to formulate a fundamental truth about religions, she overlooks their particular histories and the incompatibility of many of their tenets. For example, Jesus is deprived of His divine nature. H. D. sees Him as an ideal man rather than as the Son of God and Redeemer of man. He becomes a paradigm of spiritual growth and a supreme hero, but He loses His role as God incarnate. Similarly, she levels moral principles, theological distinctions, and devotional practices; in their place she advocates a universalist mysticism. History, philosophy, and theology yield to wordplay and occultism. The result is spiritual iconoclasm: religions tumbling at the impulse of her will and "intuitions."

Although the reader may be dismayed by H. D.'s theology, his sympathy is almost certain to be aroused by the candor and intensity of her quest for a religious experience. Her need for a relationship with God is so obvious that, regardless of the persuasiveness of her claims, one rejoices that she felt encouraged in her quest. Ironically, the reader may be inclined to mingle good will and condescension toward her in the same way that she did toward Freud.

III By Avon River

The finest fruit of H. D.'s sense of spiritual rebirth during the war years is *By Avon River*, published in 1949 but written in 1945-46. It is a small volume consisting of two parts: a poem "Good Frend" and an essay "The Guest." They are graceful pieces occasioned by the poetry of the English Renaissance and imbued with H. D.'s faith in the existence of a loving Spirit behind the turmoil of human affairs.

"Good Frend" marks a visit to Stratford on Shakespeare Day, 1945. The title comes from Shakespeare's burial plea: "Good frend for Jesus sake forbeare,/To digg the dust encloased heare!/Bleste be the man that spares thes stones,/And curst be he that moves my bones." The piece is arranged in tightly knit, unrhymed stanzas of varying lengths, in which H. D.'s voice merges with those of several fictitious ones. She begins the poem with an unusually successful play on words: "Come as you will, but I came home/Driven by *The Tempest*" (5). Literally, the entire poem is a meditation upon the imagined character of Claribel, mentioned in *The Tempest* merely as the daughter of the King of Naples and recently wed at Tunis. Figuratively, the tempest is World War II, just then in its final days. As Shakespeare's play presents the moral regeneration of miscreants by means of a violent storm, H. D. speaks of the insight that has been born of her spiritual victory over violence. "Home" is Stratford, the poet's native village and place of retirement; more generally, it is everyman's peaceful haven. While H. D. waits in line to enter the church where Shakespeare is buried, she wonders what the image of Claribel may have meant to him when, after a busy career in the theater, he composed his last play. Shakespeare's reticence spurs her imagination, and she decides that Shakespeare saw in Claribel the noblest embodiment of love.

The second part, "Rosemary," is an ode upon flowers—and Claribel—as symbols of immortality. H. D. tells of entering the church and waiting in line to touch the letters of Shakespeare's epitaph. She recalls, "If I could touch the stone, I knew/That virtue would go out of it" (10). However, when she reached the grave, she discovered that the stone was invisible under flowers. This surprise led her to rejoice that "the power/Of Love transformed Death to a flower" (11). She honors "the sweet herb,/Rosemary" (12) above all the other plants. As the traditional adornment of both the wedding gown and the shroud, it reminds her of the fusion of love and immortality. Also, she finds it appropriate for Shakespeare because its woody stem may be associated with the lute of his poetry and the sturdy construction of his plays: "O, what a house he built/To shelter all of us" (13). Finally, the name "rosemary" reminds H. D. of *ros maris*, the sea rose, which in turn reminds her of the sea change wrought upon the fortunes and the moral condition of many of Shakespeare's characters.

She returns to pondering why the "invisible, voiceless Claribel" (14) moves her so deeply, why Shakespeare chose this evocative name and why he wrote no more than that she had "a sweet marriage." She decides that the absence of detail enhances Claribel's appeal; not limited by any particular situation, the name is free to stir the imagination as a symbol of spiritual fulfillment. H. D. wonders what consolation this fancied creature may have brought to Shakespeare during his last days:

> What voice it was from Avallon,
> Calling that last April,
> *Farewell, farewell,*
> *But only to pain, regret, disaster,*
> *O friend, farewell*
> *Is only to fear, despair, torture,*
> *Say not farewell,*
> *But hail, Master.*
> Was it Ariel?
> Was it Claribel? (17)

H. D.'s responsiveness to this image is most fully demonstrated in the final section of the poem, "Claribel's Way to God." In a dramatic monologue, Claribel explains how her life has been spent. Although she is the Queen of Tunis, she has always been drawn to the spiritual life. She first tried the life of the Poor Clares but found it counter to her vocation. Then she became a nursing sister in Venice, caring for knights wounded on the Crusades. There, one knight had the spiritual insight to penetrate her temporal role. He saw in her the incarnation of spiritual love: "I laid the spray upon his tunic,/He said, ah Mary, nay, not Mary,/But Wisdom, the Supernal Light;/The trouvères hid in the aubade, . ." (23). For him, she was the Lady of the troubadors' love songs—no actual woman but a divine spirit worshipped in the guise of a woman. Looking into her eyes, he enjoyed a vision of Paradise. When the monologue ends, H. D. finds herself kneeling "in Avon meadow" (24). The knight's recognition of Claribel's identity confirms H. D.'s understanding of Shakespeare's image and strengthens her own faith in the transcendent value of love. She sees more clearly now: "How Love is God, how Love is strong,/When One is Three and Three are One,/The Dream, the Dreamer and the Song" (25).

In "The Guest," which pays homage to the poets of the English Renaissance, H. D. offers her impression of virtually every poet from the time of Shakespeare's birth to the Civil War, with the exception of Milton, who, she explains, is omitted out of respect for his greatness. The essay is a personal appreciation, not a critical discussion. She simply tells what has impressed her about each author: "We wander through a labyrinth. If we cut straight through, we destroy the shell-like curves and involutions. Where logic is, where reason dictates, we have walls, broad highways, bridges, causeways. But we are in a garden" (34). The fragmentary and subjective nature of the piece is both its charm and its limitation. She aims at a "living and personal memory" (43), let historians say what they will.

Although her approach is random and desultory, it is directed by two firm attitudes. The first is her delight in the lyric verse of the Renaissance. She quotes generously from the loveliest of poems and comments enthusiastically upon their artistry. She especially admires their musicality: "Every gentleman at the Court of Henry VIII, was, like the king himself, musician and poet. Music and poetry were not yet disassociated" (72). Her comments bespeak a lifetime of pleasure in Renaissance lyricism and suggest a facet of her own work that may be obscured by her use of free verse.

The second unifying feature of the essay is its theme. Although she discusses fifty-nine poets and turns her attention to numerous subjects, one attitude is dominant throughout. It is suggested by the title-poem, "The Guest"—Raleigh's lyric written during his imprisonment in the Tower:

> Go, Soul, the Body's guest,
>   Upon a thankless arrant,
> Fear not to touch the best;
>   The truth shall be thy warrant;
>   Go, since I needs must die,
>   And give the World the lie!
>
> Say to the Court, it glows
>   And shines like rotten wood;
> Say to the Church, it shows
>   What's good and doth no good;
>   If Church and Court reply,
>   Then give them both the lie.

Like Raleigh in this poem, H. D. celebrates the autonomy of the soul and its ability to outlast temporal adversity. She refers repeatedly to the horror of life in Elizabethan and Jacobean England—the religious and political persecutions, the outbursts of warfare, and the plague—in order to show the poets transcending the caprice and cruelty of fortune. Some, of course, became cynical, but H. D. believes that the finest of them "gave the lie" to misfortune. Although their allegiance to the Court and the Church was sapped, loyalty to their faith in the invulnerability of the soul grew stronger. Their resignation to the brevity of life was stark; for example, there are Nash's "Come, come the bells do cry;/I am sick, I must die" and Shirley's: "The glories of our blood and state/Are shadows, not substantial things;/There is no armour against Fate;/Death lays his icy hand on kings."

Countering this grim consciousness was the triumphant spirituality expressed in Donne's "Death, thou shalt die." The spiritual ardor of these poets showed most brilliantly in love poetry, either in the earthly love of Herrick's "Bid Me to Live" or in the ecstatic love of Crashaw's poem to Saint Teresa. H. D. sees in both types equally fervid continuations of the "Religion of Love" of the troubadors. These poets used terrestrial language, but their motive was to express the union of the soul with the Absolute.

In the course of expressing this theme, H. D. offers numerous opinions about Renaissance English poetry and the lives of the poets. The reader may resist some of them, but even disagreement should not reduce his enjoyment because H. D.'s goal is merely "to recall echoes of the great period" (69). The charm of the essay is her intense delight in the poetry of a bygone era.

CHAPTER 7

Helen in Egypt

HELEN IN EGYPT,[1] published in 1961, is H. D.'s most ambitious work. It is a book-length poem divided into three sections and written in three-line stanzas of free verse; each section consists of "Books" that are introduced by a prose commentary. The poem is a dramatic monologue by Helen of Troy (a few other voices are also heard); the prose commentator, H. D., anticipates the reader's questions and directs his responses.

Helen's monologue concentrates upon her experiences during the Trojan War, particularly upon her seduction by Paris and the fall of the House of Priam; but allusions are also made to the entire landscape of Greek myth and legend. The title refers to H. D.'s variation upon the traditional story: instead of being taken to Troy by Paris, Helen spends the war years in Egypt. H. D., tracing this innovation to Stesichorus, a Greek poet of the sixth century B.C., explains that "according to the *Pallinode* [by Stesichorus], Helen was never in Troy. She had been transposed or translated from Greece into Egypt. Helen of Troy was a phantom, substituted for the real Helen, by jealous deities. The Greeks and the Trojans alike fought for an illusion" (1). Another departure from the tradition, although also based upon classical sources, is the romance of Helen and Achilles.[2] After the war, Helen is joined in Egypt by Achilles, not Menelaus. At first Achilles is full of rage at the woman who has caused the ten years of war, but his wrath changes to love as they recognize that they have been destined for each other. In the main, the poem is Helen's reflection upon the meaning of this unexpected development. Her inquiry leads her to raise several other important issues; for example, the differences between Egyptian and Greek culture and the need for a reconciliation between the Greeks and the Trojans. But these are incidental to her effort to fathom the destiny that has bound her to the Greek hero.

Her conclusion—the theme of the poem—is stark and transcendental: the perfect love that she and Achilles seek is to be found in death: "the dart of Love/is the dart of Death" (314). Achilles' death at Troy enables him to overcome the distraction of earthly power: "some said a bowman from the Walls/let fly the dart, some said it was Apollo,/but I, Helena, know it was Love's arrow; . ." (9). Transfigured by death, he becomes "the new Mortal" (10), an immortal lover, for Helen claims that it is "only the true immortals/who partake of mortality" (29). She sees that her fate is linked to his. The most beautiful woman and the mightiest warrior are to be immortalized by accepting the fatal wound of love. She believes that love is "one finite moment" (314) that leads to death and rebirth in eternity.

The implications of this theme for H. D. are far from clear. Both the subject and her way of presenting it create difficulties for the reader. Transcendental intuitions are ineffable; as their nature surpasses mundane limits, efforts to describe them overtax the strength of words. The substance that ordinarily serves as the common ground between writer and reader is reduced to an airy mystery. Moreover, in this case, H. D. launches her transcendental flights from the uncertain base of Greek mythology. The incidents of the Trojan War are, for the modern reader, shadows projected over many centuries from a congeries of literary sources. It is difficult to respond to H. D.'s allusions because the territory to which they refer is uncertain. The reader feels that H. D. brings a lifetime of passionate involvement with classical antiquity to every detail in the poem, but he cannot be sure that his response is in tune with her passion. He fears that Helen's remarks sometimes carry overtones that he either fails to hear or misunderstands.

The insubstantiality of the theme is compounded by the nebulous details of the action. Events take place in an unearthly atmosphere. For example, the reader wonders which characters, if any, are alive. Is Achilles dead when he meets Helen in Egypt; did Helen die at Troy (the phantom Helen, that is); does Helen in Egypt have any greater reality than Helen in Troy, and is the entire discourse only a dream—the dream of a phantom?

Adding to these perplexities about the substantiality of the characters and the action are the oracular statements made throughout the poem, particularly those about Helen's desire to "know the Sun,/hidden behind the sun of our visible day" (35). Helen in Egypt is said to be "both phantom and reality" (3). Although she seems preoccupied with the outcome of the Trojan

War, at one point she asks, "What does it matter,//who won, who lost?" (37). Similarly, opaque answers are given to questions like, "How are Helen in Egypt/and Helen upon the ramparts,/together yet separate?" (65) and "How reconcile Trojan and Greek?" (163). The reader is told, "Seek not to know//too much" (109), and "What is thought/to forgetting?" (175). Assurance is also given that "Helen understands, though we do not know exactly what it is that she understands" (198); and, in the concluding passage of the poem, that "one greater than Helen must answer, though perhaps we do not wholly understand the significance of the Message" (314).

The motive behind these statements is apparent: H. D. wishes to unsettle the reader's assumptions about reality. Her aim is to stir transcendental intuitions, not to tell an adventure story about the Trojan War. By blurring the border between the known and the unknown, she hopes to make the reader aware of unsuspected cosmic dimensions. He is to see matter and time as phases of spirit and eternity. The implications of love and death are to include the Absolute. The Trojan War, the beauty of Helen, and the vulnerability of Achilles are to function as symbols of perennial spiritual forces. In carrying out this intention, surety and definiteness would be signs of failure. Her opalescent style is at least a warrant that she has not oversimplified her task.

Unfortunately, the reader is apt to be confused by her effort to adumbrate the sublime. The absence of fixed narrative and dramatic details may simply be baffling. In being spared any pedestrian distractions, he may be rendered unable to respond positively to the theme at all. To minimize such confusion, the three sections of the poem—"Pallinode," "Leuké," and "Eidolon" —should be discussed successively. This procedure demonstrates that H. D. establishes her theme early in the poem and then expands and intensifies its implications. There is no advance in time from beginning to end but a deepening of meaning—a lyrical rather than a narrative progression.

I *"Pallinode"*

The title of the first section refers to a poem by Stesichorus in which he offers—according to H. D.—"a defence, explanation or apology" (1) for an earlier attack upon Helen. Apparently, the Greeks' disappointment over Helen's becoming the mistress of a Trojan conflicted with their love of her beauty. To overcome this conflict, Stesichorus altered the legend so that Helen is miraculously transported from Sparta to Egypt and, unknown to Paris, only a phantom accompanies him to Troy. By adopting Stesichorus' title, H. D. indicates that she accepts his version of the tradition and wishes to rehabilitate Helen's reputation. Actually, the issue of Helen's real presence either in Troy or in Egypt is largely ignored. Because the poet's interests are metaphysical, locating her characters in a definite time and place is of little importance to her.

For H. D., Egypt stands primarily for a mode of understanding. She presents Helen in the temple of Amen, surrounded by lotus emblems and hieroglyphics. Helen finds that in Egypt "the old enchantment holds" (2); that is, eternal patterns are figured in the ancient symbols. Her task is to translate her particular situation "into timeless-time or hieroglyph or ancient Egyptian time" (13) so that its transcendental meaning may be grasped. She realizes that the vehicle for acquiring such knowledge is different from the rational mode of Greece; it is "intuitive or emotional knowledge, rather than intellectual" (13). Helen is said to have acquired this knowledge—"the heart accepts,//encompasses the whole/of the undecipherable script" (89)—but because she is a Hellene, she wishes to conceptualize it. Ultimately, she aspires to "bring Egypt and Greece together" (83).

Helen has found peace in Egypt by recognizing that "God does not weave a loose web" (85). She believes that no happening, however slight, lies outside His purpose. More specifically, she is convinced that the strange events of her life have been governed by the principle that "Love should be born of War" (33). For her, the ten years' agony at Troy occurred "in order that two souls or two soul-mates should meet" (5). Addressing her thoughts to the Greek warriors who cursed her when she appeared upon the Trojan ramparts, she says:

you are forgiven, for I know my own,
and God for his own purpose
wills it so, that I

stricken, forsaken draw to me,
through magic greater than the trial of arms,
your own invincible, unchallenged Sire,

Lord of your legions, King of Myrmidons,
unconquerable, a mountain and a grave,
Achilles; . . . (5-6)

Alone in the temple, she meditates upon her meeting with Achilles. She decides that his death at Troy was accomplished by "Love's arrow" (9): "it was God's plan/to melt the icy fortress of the soul,/and free the man" (10). An old man in "a strange ship" (59) carried him to Egypt, where Helen met him—"the new Mortal" (10)—at the shore. At first he was astonished to find her there: "what sort of enchantment is this? . . . are you a witch? . . . am I a ghost?" She replied, "You are living, O child of Thetis,/as you never lived before" (16). Still associating her with the war, he accused her of causing the death of many Greek heroes. When she called the Trojan War merely a "dream and a phantasy," he attacked her "with his fingers' remorseless steel" (17). Fortunately, in her distress she cried out to his mother Thetis for the strength to accept her fate; her prayer struck Achilles with the force of a revelation, causing him to submit to the destiny that "brought Helen/to sleep in his arms" (20).

Throughout the remainder of "Pallinode," Helen tries to understand the shocking events that form the background to her union with Achilles. Mostly she is alone, although in one sequence Achilles joins her in the temple and describes the horror of the war. He also admits that his love for her began at Troy when their eyes met as she walked the rampart. Despite his antagonism toward her, he recognized then that "all things would change but never/the glance she exchanged with me" (56). Helen's thoughts fix upon the misfortunes of her family, especially Clytaemnestra. She sees that she and Achilles are involved in the calamity of her sister's life. When the Greek forces gathered at Aulis to avenge Paris' abduction of Helen, they were becalmed until Iphigenia, the daughter of Agememnon and Clytaemnestra, was sacrificed. The girl was tricked into coming to Aulis by the pretense that Achilles wanted to marry her. Clytaemnestra hated Agamemnon for consenting to his daughter's death, and soon after was unfaithful to him. Thus began the series of violent deeds that led to her being slain by her son Orestes. Helen ponders these happenings: "why should Helen be given/peace through eternity,/and Clytaemnestra doomed, . ." (72).

Although she even wonders if these events might merely be dreams, her strongest inclination is to accept them as part of God's inscrutable and ultimately beneficent plan. The hieroglyphics help her to reach this conclusion. She merges the characters of Egyptian and Greek mythology and relates them to her situation. Achilles is both Osiris and Typhon, his brother and destroyer; Thetis is linked to Isis, Aphrodite, and even Helen herself; the Greek army is cognate to Horus and Eros. The result of these multiple associations is to enable Helen to accept everything that has happened as inevitably patterned in eternity. Her mind cannot perceive the harmony in such a labyrinth, but

> the heart does not wonder?
> the heart does not ask?
> the heart accepts,
>
> encompasses the whole
> of the undecipherable script. . . . (89)

The peace that Helen finds in seeing the events of her life as predestined is compromised by its dependence upon her isolation in the temple. Apparently, her serenity is possible only when she is alone with the sacred hieroglyphics; it cannot endure contact with the world. Even Achilles is absent, although their love is the keystone to her happiness. Indeed, it is doubtful that he has yet been with her in more than a spiritual sense. The dream-like quality of the entire setting—its location in "timeless-time"—suggests that her reconciliation of love, war, and her personal fate has occurred in a vision. She is startled to think that she has entered a realm of phantoms: "Have I imprisoned myself//in my contemplation?/has my happiness set me apart/from the rest of Egypt?" (92). She is grateful for the spiritual consolation she has received, but she dislikes having to experience it in solitude, apart from the world of time and circumstance:

> can we take our treasure,
>
> the wisdom of Amen and Thoth,
> back to the islands,
> that enchantment may find a place
>
> where desolation ruled,
> and a warrior race,
> Agamemnon and Menelaus? (93)

Help in resolving this problem is provided her. The final part of "Pallinode" is a statement attributed to an "Image or Eidolon" of Achilles' mother Thetis. Just as her name had enabled Helen to withstand Achilles' initial attack, Thetis now tells Helen how the intuitions she has experienced in Egypt may enrich her life.

She urges Helen to accept the fate that has united her to Achilles and to refrain from questioning the will of God by worrying about her sister's fate—"God willed that Helena/be joined to Achilles,/that Clytaemnestra//be called to another Star" (106). Finally, Thetis challenges Helen to give up her solitary ecstasy in Egypt and return to waking reality. She reminds Helen that "the timeless, hieratic symbols can be paralleled with symbols in-time" (111). Objects in nature convey wisdom no less relevant than that of the hieroglyphics: "a simple spiral-shell may tell/a tale more ancient/than these mysteries; . ." (111). She counsels Helen to "dare the uncharted seas" in order to go where "Achilles waits, and life" (111). Her plea, "Helen—come home" (112), brings the "Pallinode" to a close.

II *"Leuké"*

The second section, "Leuké," is titled after an island in the Black Sea where, H. D. remarks, "Achilles is said to have married Helen who bore him a son, Euphorion" (113). Although H. D. mentions this detail at the outset, it has no thematic significance; it merely accounts for her choice of this setting. More pertinent is the subtitle, "*L'isle blanche.*" The whiteness of the island signifies daylight, the world of time. The commentator explains that "Helen in Egypt . . . was in an ecstatic or semi-trance state. . . . Now, it is as if momentarily, at any rate, the dream is over. Remembrance is taking its place" (113). The change in consciousness is figured in the imagery of a sea journey, like Achilles' journey to Egypt. She can remember only the stars and a skiff, but she is glad to be in the new atmosphere: "I can not endure the weight of eternity,/. . ./. . . I am free" (114).

Once more in a waking state, she is willing to postpone her promised meeting with Achilles until the ghosts of her past have been laid. This commitment puts her "back with the old dilemma—who caused the war?" (115). She recognizes that a crucial step was taken when Achilles' mother Thetis married the mortal Peleus and failed to invite Eris to the wedding celebration. Eris retaliated by throwing a golden apple marked "to the fairest" amid the assembled guests. This challenge led to the judgment of Paris, the abduction of Helen, and the war. However, Helen reminds herself that the chain of causality may always be traced link by link endlessly; she turns more realistically to the decisive figure with whom she is involved—Paris: "he was banished, as his mother dreamed/that he (Paris) would cause war,/and war came" (114). She recognizes also that, although Achilles was slain by "Love's arrow, . . . it was Paris who was the agent, medium or intermediary of Love" (116).

At this point, Paris appears to Helen. He speaks of the fall of Troy, his own death, and of his undying love for her. He recalls that after he shot the arrow that felled Achilles, he had been mortally wounded by Philoctetes, thus ending his brief reign as king. As he lay dying, the city was demolished. He watched as fire destroyed the turrets and ramparts, leaving only a fragment of a wall as his kingdom. More significantly, he says that he watched Helen trying to flee to safety. He insists that the various accounts by poets about her miraculous delivery from the doomed city are false: "I am the first in all history/to say, she died, died, died/when the Walls fell; . ." (135).

Convinced of Helen's death, Paris has been awaiting her resurrection; and now, finding her on Leuké, he believes that it has occurred. He immediately pleads for the revival of their love. To prove his fidelity, he says that he refused his wife Oenone's offer to cure his wound if he would forget Helen. Then after his death, Aphrodite promised to restore him to life—on the same condition. Once more he refused. He has been steadfast in his love, and he now hopes to be requited. Unfortunately, he is not able to uproot Achilles from her heart, although he tries desperately: "He was never your lover" (144), "why remember Achilles?" (147), and:

> you say I have recalled the past,
> and for that past, there was only one healing
> (appeasement, death or awakening,
>
> anodyne, incense) for the initiate,
> (after the inevitable sequence of long tortures,
> long waiting), the Mysteries of Egypt;
>
> you say you did not die on the stairs,
> that the love of Achilles sustained you;
> I say he never loved you. (149)

However, Helen rejects his appeal and departs from him.

Exhausted by her encounter with Paris, Helen turns for support to the legendary hero Theseus. He is her "god-father"—a surrogate for the human father she does not have. When she was a child, Theseus stole her from Sparta. In time she became fond of him, and although she was later rescued by her brothers, she retained a feeling of kinship for him and trusted his counsel. Now she appears before him—the setting is unclear; it may be Leuké or Athens—"baffled and buffeted and very tired" (157). He welcomes her and is willing to be of help, but he warns that his understanding of love has grown weak. He believes that only a transcendent experience remains indelible and that his touch with the Absolute occurred on "the Quest and the Argo" rather than with "Love, the Immortal" (155).

Helen tells him why she is distressed: her decision to leave the isolated serenity of Egypt has confronted her with the problems of her past—"I wanted to come home,/I found Paris" (159). She describes her desire for Hellenic scenes:

> I found perfection in the Mysteries,
> but I was home-sick for familiar trees,
> I wanted to hear the wind, to feel
>
> snow, to embrace an ancient
> twisted pine, so I walked
> a long way up a mountain
>
> he called Ida; . . . (160)

Theseus says that she must neither resume a disembodied existence in Egypt nor continue worrying about the claims of the past. He asserts that she really is seeking not Achilles nor Paris but a divine Lover: "beyond Trojan and Greek//is the cloud, the wind, the Lover/you sought in the snow; . ." (172). He tells her that the way to this Lover is through death. As he risked death with the Minotaur in order to gain the stature of a hero, she must reach her Lover by surrendering to death. He assures her that the outcome will be a fulfillment not an annihilation: "there is nothing to fear,/you are neither there nor here,//but wavering/like a Psyche/with half-dried wings" (173).

She accepts his counsel, for death holds no terror for her. The commentator remarks that Helen realizes "the Absolute of negation, if you will, or of completion . . . and hence in a sense, of Death" (203). She herself declares, "But now, only the memory of the molten ember/of the Dark Absolute claims me//who have met Death,/who have found Dis,/who embraced Hades" (204). However, she identifies the divine Lover waiting beyond death with Achilles. Every mortal detail of life may be forgotten but "never, never . . . Achilles" (178). She insists that he is not a distraction from fulfillment but the fulfillment itself—the Golden Fleece of her Quest for Love. Her visions of him have been warrants of the perfect union they shall enjoy eternally.

Seeing Achilles as her divine Lover helps her to come to peace with two great anxieties: her involvement with war and her relationship with Paris. She learns that War, Death, and Love are part of an eternal pattern of Darkness. But this pattern is not the only one; Theseus figures in an alternate one of Light, Life, and Victory. The two patterns lead to the Absolute by different paths: "Achilles vanquished before Troy,//Theseus, ever-victorious." To the question, "How have the arcs crossed?/how have the paths met?" (196), the commentator answers that "they meet as opposites meet, dark-light, life-death, death-life and so on. They meet finally in 'Helen in Egypt' and 'Helen in Hellas forever'" (197).

Confident that she now understands the pattern of War and Death of which she is a part, Helen is able to reconcile her involvement with Paris and her transcendent destiny with Achilles. She sees Paris as a foreshadowing of her greater lover—"Paris was my youth—don't you see?/must youth and maturity quarrel?" (188). Surprisingly, Paris is then transformed into a symbol of Eros because he is loved by Aphrodite and because he first awakened Helen to love. Next, on the assumption that love is born of War and Death for those people destined to the pattern of Darkness, Paris is seen as the child of Helen and Achilles. Thus Paris is not spurned; his role is to unite his beloved with his enemy. Helen rejoices, "I lost the Lover, Paris,/but to find the Son" (161). Later, making a deserved concession to incredulity, she says:

> he of the House of the Enemy,
> Troy's last king (this is no easy thing
> to explain, this subtle genealogy)
>
> is Achilles' son, he is incarnate
> Helen-Achilles; he, my first lover,
> was created by my last; . . . (191-92)

In this fashion, Helen harmonizes her temporal and eternal roles, as well as the hostility between the Trojans and the Greeks.

Having achieved this extraordinary integration, "Helen is at peace, she has found the answer, she will rest" (201). Conflicts are past; now she wishes only to realize more fully the meaning of their resolution: "I must have time to remember/Dis, Hades, Achilles" (207). She stands on the border of time and eternity; "her cycle in time" (208) is finished. Before entering a timeless plane, she wishes to "encompass the infinite/in time, in the crystal,/in my thought here" (209). Naturally, Achilles is the center of her meditation. She remembers the promise of Thetis—"Achilles waits"—and concludes that it refers to his being obliged to "finish his task,/Hercules' twelve labours" (210) around the Wheel of the Zodiac before they may be united. For her, "the Wheel is still" (211), but she says:

I would wander through the temples
of the stars, his familiars;
I would seek, I would find,

I would endure with him,
the twelve labours,
conquer Boar, Stag, Lion; . . . (214)

Recognizing that this wish may be inordinate, she concludes her meditation more humbly with the "one prayer,/may he find the way" (215).

III *"Eidolon"*

The title "Eidolon" refers to an apparition or image of Achilles' mother, the sea goddess Thetis, who is identified also with love goddesses, mother goddesses, and with death. Bearing these multiple associations, Thetis symbolizes the theme of the poem—the metamorphosis resulting from submitting oneself unreservedly to Love. She is the idol, "a wooden doll/that Thetis' child hid away" (302), that guides Achilles and Helen ultimately to their destiny, despite their personal anxieties and the efforts of others to deflect them from their goal.

Helen is brought back to Egypt at the wish of Achilles, who appears now "not as Lord of Legions, 'King of Myrmidons,' but as one dedicated to a new Command, that of the 'royal sacred High Priest of love-rites'" (219). He says that he is following the orders of Theseus and Amen—the earthly and spiritual manifestations of the one supreme deity. He comes upon Helen lying in a death-like state on a bier, "exhausted/with the fight . . ./to understand Leuké" (219).

Before she recovers enough to speak, Paris appears and makes a final bid for her love. He ridicules Achilles' attempt to escape the war by disguising himself as a woman, and he expresses horror at Achilles' perfidy in love: "It was not only Iphigenia,/ . . ./there was always another and another and another" (227). He calls Achilles a destroyer—"his is a death-cult" (225)—and he appeals to Helen in the name of life: "he would turn you to Pythoness,/Priestess—is there no magic//left above earth?" (226). Noticing no change in Helen's attitude, Paris surrenders to the inevitable. Seeming to recognize the futility of his own arguments, he settles for the lesser relationship previously suggested by Helen: he will accept Achilles as a father "in this new spirit-order" (226) if Helen will be his mother.

After Paris submits to his fate, Helen experiences the fullness of her new state of consciousness. The commentator remarks:

> Helen says, "I am awake, I see things clearly; it is dawn." If the Helen of our first sequence was translated to a transcendental plane, the Amen-temple in Egypt, and the Helen of our second sequence contacted a guide or guardian, near to her in time, Theseus, the hero-king and "Master of Argo," our third Helen having realized "all myth, the one reality," is concerned with the human content of the drama. "I am awake, I see things clearly." (265)

Her thoughts turn once more to the fall of Troy. However, as she reviews "the past/in the new light of a new day" (235), the details seem unreal and unimportant. The rivalries among warriors, the battles, and the destruction of the city now resemble the elements of a play. She takes a supremely egocentric view of the drama: it has been staged in order to unite her to Achilles. The battle was an illusion wrought by Apollo to provide inspiring material to poets for all time. She is no longer certain that anything actually occurred. Her only certainty is that she has met Achilles on the Egyptian coast: "I only remember the shells, whiter than bone,/on the ledge of a desolate beach" (233).

Helen now understands Achilles' profound devotion to his mother, the sea goddess Thetis. As a child, his loneliness during Thetis' absence was solaced by a doll made in her image, an "eidolon." When he grew up, the doll was replaced by "a wooden image,/a mermaid, Thetis upon the prow" (249) of his ship. Although he had no knowledge of where she would lead him, he wanted to follow her always. In this respect, he at first found the Trojan War an unwelcome disturbance. He did not love battle, despite his prowess; his beloved was his ship—dedicated to his mother. This devotion is implied even in his being finally persuaded to join the Greeks by his desire to lead their fleet. At Aulis, he was determined to sail "with or without Iphigenia's death" because he had "promised another/white throat to a goddess" (253)—presumably a sacrifice of Helen to his mother. Later during the battle, he resumed fighting not, as the tradition goes, in order to revenge Patroclus' death but as part of a bargain whereby his mother would bring the war to a close:

> I will re-join the Greeks
> and the battle before the gate,
>
> if you promise a swift return,
> if you promise new sails for the fleet
> and a wind to bear us home, . . . (257)

When he was killed by Paris and carried to Egypt, he felt that Thetis had forsaken him. To his yet unenlightened understanding, she had "failed at last"—"she had promised him immortality/but she had forgotten to dip the heel/of the infant Achilles//into the bitter water" (262-63). Meeting Helen on the beach, his rage and disappointment led him to grip her throat in "his fingers' remorseless steel" (280). By trying to kill her, he was striking back at the entire Trojan adventure that had kept him from a happier destiny with his mother. Then Helen, acting upon an intuition, said "the word,/the one word that would turn and bind/and blind him to any other" (287)—Thetis. Suddenly Achilles realized that the grip that could take Helen's life was an embrace that would assure their immortality together.

Thetis, as the goddess of love and the sea, has determined the entire drama. She has arranged the war in order to unite Achilles and Helen. In addition, she has used the war to demonstrate that love and the sea are related to death. However, unlike ordinary death, the death suffered by lovers causes a "sea-change" that unites them forever. Perceiving this truth enabled Helen to recognize, as Achilles grasped her throat, that "this is Love, this is Death,/this is my last Lover" (278).

Throughout the remainder of the poem, Helen tries to understand more fully her union with Achilles and to resolve the conflict between the Greeks and the Trojans. At the same time, she senses the inscrutability of these mysteries: "if only God/would let me lie here forever,/I could assess, weigh and value//the secret treasure" (293). The problem is epitomized in her calling upon Thetis when Achilles seized her throat and thereby transforming his rage into love. She wonders how she happened to implore the only spirit ready to forestall her destruction. The answer is ironic: the suggestion had come from Paris. Endeavoring to turn her from Achilles, he had told her to "call on Thetis, the sea-mother" (308). In this circumstance, she finds a clue to both enigmas: she has been led to Achilles by the counsel of his rival in love and war.

As she had surmised earlier, Paris is an incarnation of Eros and thus plays a role that exceeds his mortal comprehension. As Helen and Achilles cannot alter their destiny, Paris cannot fail to lead them to it. This recognition of the inevitability of events and the connection between death, love, and regeneration is the farthest that Helen's understanding reaches. She has expressed this perception at several stages of her psychic journey; at each one it has assumed greater certitude and importance. At the close of the poem, it is presented with the authority of a revelation, although, as the commentator remarks, "perhaps we do not wholly understand the significance of the Message" (314):

so the dart of Love
is the dart of Death,
and the secret is no secret;

. . . .

the Sphinx is seen,
the Beast is slain
and the Phoenix-nest

reveals the innermost
key or the clue to the rest
of the mystery; . . . (314)

IV *Conclusion*

It is difficult to imagine readers not being moved by *Helen in Egypt*, for man's desire for absolute and eternal love seems ineradicable. To find this desire couched in the setting of the Trojan War provides a twofold satisfaction: the dramatization of both an inner need and a major episode in Western culture. The beauty of Helen, the heroism of Achilles, and the impetuosity of Paris are archetypes in which we see ourselves reflected and also catch glimpses of the past.

The persuasiveness of H. D.'s use of this material is another matter. Even a romanticist may balk at the suggestion that only through death may love be attained, and even a transcendentalist may be unable to appreciate the difference between timeless-time, ecstasy, semi-trance, dream, waking dream, and daydream. Similarly, a Hellenist who welcomes a variation upon the usual account of the Trojan War may be disappointed by the implication that the entire conflict was a phantasy planned to accomplish the union of two phantom lovers. These unusual premises might be established successfully, but it is obvious that H. D. faced many difficulties in setting about such a task.

These difficulties have not been overcome. From beginning to end, *Helen in Egypt* seems arbitrary and insubstantial. H. D. wished to present the entire poem from a supra-mundane level of consciousness, but she succeeded only in making everything appear unreal. Helen, Achilles, Theseus, Paris—all lack the grounding in reality needed to make their transcendental utterances convincing. Achilles and Helen do not seem like lovers: they show no sign of affection for each other, nor do they convey an aura of the sublime. Rather, Helen strikes the reader as the projection of a weary romantic sensibility, and Achilles as a puppet. Love is desired without any physical complications; consequently, it is predicated of spirits who are assigned the attractiveness of humanity without any of its limitations. In so far as difficulties are acknowledged, they are presented as inevitable elements in a process ultimately beneficent. Thus the ten years' battle at Troy is made part of God's plan to make soul mates of Helen and Achilles, and death is seen as a doorway to a tryst with an eternally constant lover.

These "dreams" are affecting, but only as promptings of the heart, not as the postulates of a higher knowledge. Appealing as rationalizations and wish-fulfillments, they are disturbing when offered as oracles of truth. Regrettably, H. D. overrides these distinctions and confuses metaphors of desire with mystical revelations. The reader gladly honors her imaginative rendering of deep-seated human longings, but he must recognize that she mistakes wishes for wisdom. *Helen in Egypt* expresses a religious sensibility that does not advance beyond the excitement of a self-willed euphoria.

CHAPTER 8

Evaluation

THE QUESTION that prompted this study—what has H. D. written besides a few Imagist poems found in anthologies?—has been answered. Her career spans forty-five years, from the publication of *Sea Garden* in 1916 to *Helen in Egypt* in 1961, the year of her death. Altogether she wrote more than fifteen volumes in a variety of literary forms. There are eight volumes of verse, the verse-drama *Hippolytus Temporizes*, three novels, the *Tribute to Freud, By Avon River,* and several translations, including Euripides' *Ion.*

On the basis of this total achievement, the exclusive linking of H. D. and the Imagist Movement is inaccurate. This movement came to an end by 1917, when H. D. was just beginning her career. Yet, this study has shown that, in a larger sense, the yoking of H. D. and Imagism is just. Although her intentions and her career far outdistanced Imagism, her best work lies within its orbit. H. D. is not exclusively an Imagist poet, but her best poems are Imagist.

The best ones appear in *Collected Poems* (1925)—short poems like "Storm," "Oread," "Sea Poppies," "Leda," and "Helen." They succeed for exactly the reasons that make them paradigms of Imagism. They are, in the words of the Imagist Credo, "poetry that is hard and clear, never blurred nor indefinite." In them, H. D. realizes her highest potentiality: the ability to fuse strong emotion and the imagery of nature. The images objectify her emotion, and the emotion makes the images personal. With exquisite tact, she establishes the evocative power of nature.

Calling these early lyrics H. D.'s best also entails recognizing that their stature is modest. They are excellent poems but minor in range and technique. In substance they are limited to outcries of desire for beauty and love, of scorn for complacency and compromise, and of grief at the distance between her experience and her dreams. They bespeak a strong will and a rich imagination but a narrow play of intelligence. In expressing moods varying from exhilaration to misanthropy, they strike the reader as naïvely self-centered.

After achieving recognition for these eloquent short lyrics, H. D. attempted lengthier and more complicated works. Understandably, she seems to have felt the need to bring a larger view of life to her writing. As she responded more fully to individual and social conflicts, problems of a psychological, philosophical, and even theological nature engaged her interest. Inevitably, she also turned to literary forms more appropriate than the lyric—the novel, the essay, the long meditative poem. In this way she set about making her writing an expression of wisdom, not simply of youthful idealism.

Despite these promising intentions, her later works are generally less successful than the early lyrics. Although she addressed herself to larger, more compelling themes—such as the problem of loyalty and self-interest, the problem of evil and suffering, and the existence of God—her writing became less distinguished. Whereas the hallmark of her early poems had been a luminous brevity, her later work tended to be wordy and banal. Two explanations of this change may be ventured: her preoccupation with more challenging themes may have distracted her from craftsmanship, or her experiments with the stream-of-consciousness fictional technique may have persuaded her to adopt an introspective colloquialism in her verse. In any case, her later work lacks the arresting use of language that established her reputation.

Nor is this loss in rhetorical verve matched by an increase in intellectual depth. Profound problems are raised in works like *Palimpsest*, the war poems, *Bid Me to Live*, and *Helen in Egypt*, but H. D.'s solutions are disappointing. Confrontations with personal grief and international violence are resolved either by unconvincing manipulations of events or by a vague prescription of optimistic fatalism, whereby all events—however terrifying—are accepted as part of an ultimately benign Providence. To share her confidence requires a suspension of the reader's demand for either dramatic plausibility or intellectual cogency. In this respect, H. D.'s later work resembles her earlier: both are dominated by a willfulness that either overlooks or overrides all difficulties. Conflicts are resolved the way she wants them to be. Examined closely, her certainties appear to be merely hopes stiffened by unusual self-confidence.

For these reasons, it seems right that H. D. should be remembered as an Imagist poet. Her efforts to extend her range in other directions deserve recognition, but they did not result in her finest work. Her reputation was made and will be maintained by the clarity and control of her early poems: those resembling the ones Ezra Pound praised as "straight talk, straight as the Greek." They exhibit a congruence between intention and result that satisfies the reader; no unresolved elements diminish his pleasure. Like cameos and etchings, they are excellent works of art in a minor key. Her later volumes, interesting experiments in themselves, are perhaps more important as gauges by which the superiority of her early poems may be measured.

Notes and References

Chapter One

1. H. D., *Tribute to Freud* (New York, 1956), p. 47.
2. *Ibid.*, pp. 26-27.
3. *Ibid.*, p. 39.
4. *Ibid.*, p. 50.
5. *Ibid.*, p. 49.
6. *Ibid.*, p. 23.
7. *Ibid.*, pp. 161-62.
8. Letter from H. D., quoted in Glenn Hughes, *Imagism and the Imagists* (Stanford, 1931), p. 110.
9. Thomas B. Swann, *The Classical World of H. D.* (Lincoln, Nebraska, 1962), p. 10.
10. Douglas Bush, *Mythology and the Romantic Tradition in English Poetry* (New York, 1963).
11. William Carlos Williams, *The Autobiography of William Carlos Williams* (New York, 1948), pp. 67-68.
12. Hughes, pp. 110-11.
13. Ezra Pound, *Literary Essays of Ezra Pound*, ed. and intro. T. S. Eliot (Norfolk, Conn., 1954), p. 11.
14. Ezra Pound, *The Letters of Ezra Pound: 1907-1941*, ed. D. D. Paige (New York, 1950), p. 103.
15. Pound, *Literary Essays*, p. 58.
16. *Ibid.*, p. 19.
17. Pound, *Letters*, p. 9.
18. *Poetry*, I (October, 1912), 31.
19. *Poetry*, I (November, 1912), 64.
20. See note 8 above.
21. Stanley K. Coffman, Jr., *Imagism: A Chapter for the History of Modern Poetry* (Norman, Okla., 1951).
22. *Ibid.*, p. 3.
23. *Poetry*, I (November, 1912), 65.
24. Hughes, p. 111.
25. Richard Aldington, *Life for Life's Sake* (New York, 1941), pp. 135-36.
26. Pound, *Letters*, p. 11.
27. *Poetry*, I (January, 1913), 135.
28. S. Foster Damon, *Amy Lowell* (Boston, 1935), p. 196.
29. *Poetry*, I (January, 1913), 126.
30. Hughes, p. 26.
31. *Poetry*, I (March, 1913), 201-2.
32. *Des Imagistes: An Anthology* (New York, 1914).
33. Letter from Pound to Harriet Monroe, quoted in Harriet Monroe, *A Poet's Life* (New York, 1938), p. 367.
34. Monroe, p. 367.
35. John Cournos, *Autobiography* (New York, 1935), pp. 268-69.
36. Damon, p. 240.

37. *Some Imagist Poets: An Anthology* (Boston, 1915).
38. *Ibid.*, pp. vi-vii.
39. *The Egoist*, III (June, 1916), 85.
40. William Carlos Williams, *Selected Essays of William Carlos Williams* (New York, 1954), pp. 9-10.
41. Damon, p. 405.
42. *D. H. Lawrence: A Composite Biography*, ed. Edward Nehls (3 vols.; Madison, Wis., 1957-59), I, 447.
43. *D. H. Lawrence*, III, 98.
44. Coffman, p. 31.
45. Harry T. Moore, *The Intelligent Heart: The Story of D. H. Lawrence* (New York, 1954), p. 248.
46. Aldington, pp. 206-7.
47. Bryher, *The Heart to Artemis* (New York, 1962), p. 182.
48. *Ibid.*, p. 186.
49. *Tribute to Freud*, pp. 59-60.

Chapter Two

1. H. D., *Collected Poems of H. D.* (New York, 1925). *Sea Garden* remained intact, except that the two final poems—"Cities" and "The City Is Peopled"—were combined and called "Cities," and "Pear Tree" was added. *Hymen* was left untouched, although "Not Honey" was retitled "Fragment 113." *Heliodora and Other Poems* was called simply *Heliodora*; and from this volume, one poem—"Odyssey"—was excluded. Six other poems—"Oread," "The Pool," "Moonrise," "Sitalkas," "Hermonax," and "Orion Dead"—with five new poems—"The God," "Adonis," "Pygmalion," "Eurydice," and "The Tribute"—were added to form a new section, *The God*, which was placed after *Sea Garden*.
2. H. D., *Selected Poems*, ed. Norman Holmes Pearson (New York, 1957).
3. Pound, *Letters*, p. 11.
4. Aldington, pp. 138-39.
5. Bryher, p. 189.
6. R. P. Blackmur, "The Lesser Satisfactions," *Poetry*, XLI (November, 1932), 100.
7. Swann, p. 173.
8. Bush, p. 505.
9. Horace Gregory and Marya Zaturenska, *A History of American Poetry: 1900-1940* (New York, 1942), p. 192.
10. Harriet Monroe, *Poets and Their Art* (New York, 1932), pp. 92-93.
11. Babette Deutsch, *Poetry in Our Time* (New York, 1956), p. 98.
12. Amy Lowell, *Tendencies in Modern American Poetry* (New York, 1917), p. 279.

Chapter Three

1. H. D., *Palimpsest* (Paris, 1926). In the same year, this edition was reprinted by the Houghton Mifflin Company. Page references are applicable to either edition.
2. H. D., *Hedylus* (Boston, 1928). Page references are to this edition.

3. H. D., *Bid Me to Live* (New York, 1960). Page references are to this edition.
4. Aldington, pp. 207, 229-33.
5. Cournos, pp. 283, 297-99, 327.
6. *D. H. Lawrence: A Composite Biography*, I, 447; III, 70, 98.

Chapter Four

1. H. D., *Red Roses for Bronze* (London, 1931).

Chapter Five

1. Pound, *Literary Essays*, p. 249.
2. *Ibid.*, p. 273.
3. Ezra Pound, *Personae of Ezra Pound* (New York, n.d.), p. 207.
4. Ezra Pound, *The Translations of Ezra Pound*, introd. Hugh Kenner (London, 1953), p. 10.
5. R. P. Blackmur, "Masks of Ezra Pound," *Form and Value in Modern Poetry* (Garden City, N.Y., 1957), p. 90.
6. H. D., *Euripides' Ion, Translated with Notes* (Boston, 1937). Page references are to this edition.
7. T. S. Eliot, "Euripides and Professor Murray," *Selected Essays* (New York, 1950), p. 47.
8. *Ibid.*, p. 49.
9. *Ibid.*, p. 50.
10. Henry Rushton Fairclough, *The Classics and Our Twentieth-Century Poets* (Stanford, 1927), p. 36.
11. *Ibid.*, p. 31.
12. *Ibid.*, p. 32.
13. *Ibid.*, p. 34.
14. *Ibid.*, p. 36.
15. Bush, p. 497.
16. *Ibid.*, p. 498.
17. *Ibid.*
18. *Ibid.*, p. 500.
19. *Ibid.*
20. *Ibid.*, p. 501.
21. Richard Lattimore, "Euripides as Lyrist," *Poetry*, LI (December, 1937), 160-64.
22. *Ibid.*, p. 162.
23. *Ibid.*, p. 161.
24. *Ibid.*, p. 162.
25. *Ibid.*, p. 163.
26. *Ibid.*
27. *Ibid.*, p. 164.
28. *Ibid.*
29. H. D., *Hippolytus Temporizes* (Boston, 1927). Page references are to this edition.
30. R. P. Blackmur, "Ritual," *Hound and Horn*, I (September, 1927), 50.

Chapter Six

1. H. D., *The Walls Do Not Fall* (London, 1944). Page references are to this edition.
2. H. D., *Tribute to the Angels* (London, 1945). Page references are to this edition.
3. H. D., *The Flowering of the Rod* (London, 1946). Page references are to this edition.
4. H. D., *By Avon River* (New York, 1949). Page references are to this edition.
5. H. D., *Tribute to Freud* (New York, 1956). Page references are to this edition.
6. Ernest Jones, "Review of H. D.'s *Tribute to Freud*," *The International Journal of Psycho-Analysis*, XXXVIII (March-April, 1957), 126.

Chapter Seven

1. H. D., *Helen in Egypt* (New York, 1961). Page references are to this edition.
2. Oskar Seyffert, *Dictionary of Classical Antiquities*, rev. and ed. Henry Nettleship and J. E. Sandys (New York, 1956), pp. 2-4, 272-73.

Selected Bibliography

PRIMARY SOURCES

1. *H. D.'s Publications:*

Sea Garden. London: Constable and Company, 1916.
Choruses from Iphigenia in Aulis. London: The Egoist Press, 1916.
Choruses from the Iphigenia in Aulis and the Hippolytus. London: The Egoist Ltd., 1919.
Hymen. London: The Egoist Press, 1921.
Heliodora and Other Poems. Boston: Houghton Mifflin, 1924.
Collected Poems of H. D. New York: Liveright Publishing Corp., 1925.
Palimpsest. Paris: Contact Editions, 1926. Also reprinted in the same year by Houghton Mifflin, Boston.
Hippolytus Temporizes. Boston: Houghton Mifflin, 1927.
Hedylus. Boston: Houghton Mifflin, 1928.
Red Roses for Bronze. London: Chatto and Windus, 1931.
The Hedgehog. London: Brendin Publishing Corp., 1936.
Euripides' Ion. Boston: Houghton Mifflin, 1937.
The Walls Do Not Fall. London: Oxford University Press, 1944.
Tribute to the Angels. London: Oxford University Press, 1945.
The Flowering of the Rod. London: Oxford University Press, 1946.
By Avon River. New York: Macmillan, 1949.
Tribute to Freud. New York: Pantheon Books, 1956.
Selected Poems of H. D. New York: Grove Press, 1957.
Bid Me to Live. New York: Grove Press, 1960.
Helen in Egypt. New York: Grove Press, 1961.

2. *Unpublished Material:*

"Special Manuscript Collection." American Literature Collection, Sterling Library, Yale University. Correspondence and manuscripts.

SECONDARY SOURCES

ALDINGTON, RICHARD. *Life for Life's Sake: A Book of Reminiscences.* New York: The Viking Press, 1941. Account by H. D.'s husband of their short married life and of the literary scene in London during World War I.

BRYHER. *The Heart to Artemis: A Writer's Memoirs.* New York: Harcourt, Brace and World, 1962. Autobiography of the historical novelist (born Winifred Ellerman), H. D.'s friend and benefactor for more than forty years.

BUSH, DOUGLAS. *Mythology and the Romantic Tradition in English Poetry.* New York: W. W. Norton, 1963. First published in 1937. Harsh evaluation of H. D.'s translations from the Greek and of her use of Hellenic subjects.

COFFMAN, STANLEY K., JR. *Imagism: A Chapter for the History of Modern Poetry.* Norman, Okla.: University of Oklahoma Press, 1951. Thorough account of the principles and personalities of the Imagist Movement.

COURNOS, JOHN. *Autobiography.* New York: G. P. Putnam's Sons, 1935. Contains a friendly account of H. D. at the time of the First World War. Refers to incidents reflected in H. D.'s novel *Bid Me to Live.*

DAMON, S. FOSTER. *Amy Lowell.* Boston: Houghton Mifflin, 1935. Contains much information about H. D. and the Imagist Movement.

DEUTSCH, BABETTE. *Poetry in Our Time.* New York: Columbia University Press, 1956. Has brief but balanced evaluation of H. D.'s work.

The Egoist: An Individualist Review. From June, 1916, to June, 1917, H. D. was the assistant editor of this important monthly periodical.

ELIOT, T. S. *Selected Essays.* New York: Harcourt, Brace, 1950. The most influential essays on contemporary poetry and culture. In "Euripides and Professor Murray," Eliot praises H. D.'s translations from Euripides.

FLETCHER, JOHN GOULD. *Life Is My Song: An Autobiography.* New York: Farrar and Rinehart, 1937. Account of his part in the Imagist Movement; contains several anecdotes about H. D.

GREGORY, HORACE, and MARYA ZATURENSKA. *A History of American Poetry: 1900-1940.* New York: Harcourt, Brace, 1942. Brief but balanced evaluation of H. D.'s early volumes.

HUGHES, GLENN. *Imagism and the Imagists.* Stanford: Stanford University Press, 1931. Survey of the Imagist Movement; separate essays on its leading members. Essay on H. D. entitled "The Perfect Imagist."

D. H. Lawrence: A Composite Biography. Gathered, arranged, and edited by EDWARD NEHLS. 3 vols. Madison, Wis.: University of Wisconsin Press, 1957-59. Volumes I and III contain important biographical material about H. D. during the First World War. Virtually the entire situation reflected in her novel *Bid Me to Live* is established.

LOWELL, AMY. *Tendencies in Modern American Poetry.* New York. Macmillan, 1917. H. D. and John Gould Fletcher are discussed in a chapter on the Imagists. Important biographical information is included.

——. (ed.). *Some Imagist Poets: An Anthology.* Boston: Houghton Mifflin, 1915. Sequels were published in 1916 and 1917. The representative collections of Imagist verse, following Pound's dissociation from the Movement. H. D. was a principal contributor.

MCALMON, ROBERT. *McAlmon and the Lost Generation: A Self-Portrait.* Edited with a commentary by ROBERT E. KNOLL. Lincoln, Neb.: University of Nebraska Press, 1962. Bryher's first husband comments briefly upon his acquaintance with H. D. in the 1920's.

MONROE, HARRIET. *Poets and Their Art.* New York: Macmillan, 1932. Founder of *Poetry Magazine* writes appreciatively of H. D.'s verse.

NORMAN, CHARLES. *Ezra Pound.* New York: Macmillan, 1960. Contains an account of H. D.'s girlhood friendship with Pound.

Poetry: A Magazine of Verse. Opening issues of *Poetry*—launched in October, 1912—contain the first public notices of Imagism and the first published verse by H. D. (in the issue of January, 1913).

POUND, EZRA. *The Letters of Ezra Pound: 1907-1941.* Edited by D. D. PAIGE. New York: Harcourt, Brace, 1950. Primary material for the history of modern poetry; contains several comments about H. D.'s imagistic verse.

———. (ed.). *Des Imagistes: An Anthology.* New York: Albert and Charles Boni, 1914. The first appearance of the Imagists as a group. H. D. was among the eleven contributors.

RIDING, LAURA, and ROBERT GRAVES. *A Survey of Modernist Poetry.* London: William Heinemann, 1927. Has brief, negative evaluation of H. D.'s verse.

DE ROUGEMONT, DENIS. *Love in the Western World.* Garden City, N.Y.: Doubleday Anchor Books, 1957. First published in 1940. A study of erotic passion; the roots of this passion are traced to mystical doctrines. H. D. regarded this book highly, and its influence is evident in her later volumes.

SWANN, THOMAS BURNETT. *The Classical World of H. D.* Lincoln, Neb.: University of Nebraska Press, 1962. Heretofore, the only book-length study of H. D. but is limited to her work on classical subjects.

WATTS, HAROLD H. "H. D. and the Age of Myth," *The Sewanee Review,* LVI (Spring, 1948), 287-303. Perceptive review of *The Walls Do Not Fall* that clarifies the attitude toward history expressed by H. D. in her later volumes.

WILLIAMS, WILLIAM CARLOS. *The Autobiography of William Carlos Williams.* New York: Random House, 1948. Several anecdotes about his friendship early in life with H. D. and Ezra Pound.

———. *Selected Essays of William Carlos Williams.* New York: Random House, 1954. In the "Prologue to *Kora in Hell,*" Williams discusses the differences between H. D. and himself over poetry and Greek literature.

Index

Index